Poverty and Litera

MW01504096

There is a mutual dependence between poverty and academic achievement, creative pedagogies for low-income pupils, school models that "beat the odds," and the resiliency of low-income families dedicated to the academic success of their children. This book examines the connection between poverty and literacy, looking at the potential roles and responsibilities of teachers, school administrators, researchers, and policymakers in closing the achievement gap and in reducing the effects of poverty on the literacy skill development of low-income children. There are numerous suggestions about how to improve schools so that they respond to the needs of low-income children; some argue for school reform, while others advocate social reform, and yet others suggest combining both educational reform and social reform.

Without a strong foundation in literacy, children are all too often denied access to a rich and diverse curriculum. Reading and writing are passports to achievement in many other curricular areas, and literacy education plays an important role in moving people out of poverty toward greater self-sufficiency post-graduation. Schools and home environments share responsibility for literacy skill development; in school, literacy equals the acquisition of reading and writing skills, but it is also a social practice key to social mobility. The achievement gap between low-income, middle-class, and upper middle-class students illustrates the power of socioeconomic factors outside school.

This book was originally published as two special issues of *Reading & Writing Quarterly: Overcoming Learning Difficulties.*

Nathalis G. Wamba is Associate Professor in the Department of Educational and Community Programs in the School of Education at Queens College, City University of New York, USA. He is co-author of *Exit Narratives: Reflections of Four Retired Teachers* (2010).

Poverty and Literacy

Edited by
Nathalis G. Wamba

 Routledge
Taylor & Francis Group

LONDON AND NEW YORK

First published in paperback 2024

First published 2012
by Routledge
4 Park Square, Milton Park, Abingdon, Oxon OX14 4RN

and by Routledge
605 Third Avenue, New York, NY 10158

Routledge is an imprint of the Taylor & Francis Group, an informa business

© 2012, 2024 Taylor & Francis

This book is a reproduction of *Reading & Writing Quarterly: Overcoming Learning Difficulties,* volume 26, issues 2-3. The Publisher requests to those authors who may be citing this book to state, also, the bibliographical details of the special issue on which the book was based.

Publisher's Note
The publisher has gone to great lengths to ensure the quality of this reprint but points out that some imperfections in the original copies may be apparent.

British Library Cataloguing in Publication Data
A catalogue record for this book is available from the British Library

ISBN: 978-0-415-69343-1 (hbk)
ISBN: 978-1-03-293045-9 (pbk)
ISBN: 978-1-315-87229-2 (ebk)

DOI: 10.4324/9781315872292

Typeset in New Times Roman
by Taylor & Francis Books

Disclaimer
The publisher would like to make readers aware that the chapters in this book are referred to as articles as they had been in the special issue. The publisher accepts responsibility for any inconsistencies that may have arisen in the course of preparing this volume for print.

Contents

Introduction

NATHALIS G. WAMBA

Queens College, City University of New York, Flushing, New York, USA

These articles collectively investigate the mutual dependence between poverty and academic achievement, creative pedagogies for low-income pupils, school models that "beat the odds," and the resiliency of low-income families dedicated to the academic success of their children. Each article also explores potential roles and responsibilities of teachers, school administrators, researchers, and policymakers in closing the achievement gap and in reducing the effects of poverty on the literacy skill development of low-income children.

Opinions abound about how to improve schools so that they respond to the needs of low-income children. There are those who argue for school reform, and others advocate social reform. Yet another group seeks to combine both educational reform and social reform. Regardless of where one falls on the continuum in relation to school reform, community reform, or both combined, comprehensive literacy education amounts to an essential component of any strategy focused on improving schools and closing the achievement gap. Without a strong foundation in literacy, children are all too often denied access to a rich and diverse curriculum. Reading and writing are passports to achievement in many other curricular areas (Kellett & Dar, 2007; Machin & McNally, 2006). Lastly, literacy education plays an important role in moving people out of poverty toward greater self-sufficiency post graduation.

Schools and home environments share responsibility for literacy skill development. In school, literacy equals the acquisition of reading and writing skills, but it is also a social practice key to social mobility (Gee, 1991). At home children develop substantial literacy skills and unique competencies through interactions with their siblings and families and through their consumption of popular culture (e.g., music, films, theater, television). Drawing upon the work of Vygotsky (1962, 1978), one can argue that effective literacy educators need to build upon (and respect) the background experiences and cultural practices of their students, especially when attempting to teach them unfamiliar academic skills and concepts.

Reading is the cornerstone of the No Child Left Behind legislation, a fundamental skill upon which formal education and access to content knowledge depend. A child who cannot read well will likely fail in school (American Federation of Teachers, 1999). If literacy skill development provides one way out of poverty, then reading and writing proficiency amounts to critical capital for children from low-income families. Longitudinal reading research demonstrates that children who do not learn to read early in their school careers invariably continue to be poor readers (Torgeson, 2000). In addition, poor readers tend to become less responsive to intervention as they grow older and their difficulties increase (Lane, Gresham, & O'Shaughnessy, 2002; Torgeson, 2000).

Ethnographic research has shed light on a wide range of culturally specific literacy practices among different communities. This research suggests that literacy involves more than just encoding and decoding symbols (Bowman, 2002; Delgado-Gaitan, 1990; Heath, 1983; Valdes, 1996). When schools integrate the cultural capital of middle- and upper middle-class children and ignore the cultural capital of other children, they ultimately end up excluding children from low-income families, preventing these children from acquiring important tools and lifelong skills that can close the achievement gap and lift them out of poverty.

From the publication of *A Nation at Risk* (National Commission on Excellence in Education, 1983) to the No Child Left Behind legislation, the U.S. public education system has gone through a series of school reforms that can be best summed up in three words: standards, accountability, and testing. Strategies to improve schools include, but are not limited to, developing new curricula and standards, providing teacher training, and fostering a better use of technology. However, the reality that factors outside school heavily constrain school reform does not receive the attention it deserves.

Educational reformers assume that if teachers know how to teach and the schools adequately support this task, children will learn irrespective of their socioeconomic status (Rothstein, 2004), a mindset that ignores the factors beyond the classroom that affect learning. Efforts focused solely on classrooms and schools could well be reversed by what takes place outside the school setting. In other words, the social, political, and economic environments in which schools exist can enable or disable school reform efforts (Berliner, 2005).

Socioeconomic factors impact academic success (see Duncan & Magnuson, 2005; Hoff, 2003; Jencks & Philips, 1998). These factors include, but are not limited to, housing, health care, the quality and accessibility of preschool, environmental stress, employment situation, and nutrition. In 2006, a representative sample of between 3,500 and 50,000 15-year-old students in 58 countries, some of them members of the Organisation for Economic Co-operation and Development (OECD), took the Program for International Students Assessment test in each country. This test focuses on the key subject areas of reading, mathematics, and science. In reading, the United States ranked 15th out of the 29 OECD countries in reading literacy, with its score of 495 coming in near the OECD average of 500 (Lemke et al., 2005). In math and science, the United States ranked 25th and 21st, respectively. Cavanagh (2007) explained that not only did many industrialized countries outperform the United States, but also that wealth, poverty, or family background mediated the academic performance of the American students to a greater extent than it did the performance of these students' peers in other higher scoring nations.

The achievement gap between low-income, middle-class, and upper middle-class students illustrates the power of socioeconomic factors outside school. Critics of this argument point to schools that beat the odds such that low-income youths have overcome barriers to their academic success. Islands of success exist, but little progress has been made to generalize these successes or to sustain them over time.

In "Children and Adolescents From Poverty and Reading Development: A Research Review," Alpana Bhattacharya explores creative pedagogies and teacher training initiatives that help teachers understand and address the effects of poverty on student achievement. This article begins with a review of literature pertinent to the decoding and reading comprehension perform-ance of struggling readers at the secondary level, particularly those from low-income backgrounds. The implications of poverty for the literacy instruction of diverse groups of students at the secondary level and in secondary content areas are also explored. Lastly, Bhattacharya describes effective instructional approaches for promoting decoding, fluency, and reading comprehension skills in secondary students who are at risk for school failure based on their low-income background.

Next, in "Race, Class, and Schooling: Multicultural Families Doing the Hard Work of Home Literacy in America's Inner City," Guofang Li draws on a larger ethnographic study to examine the literacy and cultural practices of everyday life as lived by three families of low socioeconomic status from three different racial and ethnic groups (Sudanese, Vietnamese, and White Euro-American). Li explores the complexity of reading and writing practices within each family as family members make sense of their daily relations in terms of race, ethnicity, class, and gender; as well as the production of such relations across cultural groups and within the contexts of the low-income neighborhoods and schools and the larger sociopolitical and socioeconomic formation.

Li suggests that urban education must be understood in relation to both an individual's cultural and familial milieu and the interactive context between the individual and the most powerful cultural sites, such as schools. In the current climate, minority school failure is often blamed on the deficits of disadvantaged families (and their children) and on their parenting practices that induce failure. Li, however, argues that inner city working- or under-class families are often highly literate, committed to their children's success, and capable of concerted cultivation. Yet despite ample commitment, persistence, and cultural capital, "the sticky web of institutional discourses" and the contradictions both within and between home and school cultural sites too often relegates students to failure and disadvantage.

An article by Margary Butzer, Edward Fergus, and Pedro Noguera titled "Responding to the Needs of the Whole Child: A Case Study of a High-Performing Elementary School for Immigrant Children" analyzes the strategies used by a highly successful elementary school that serves low-income immigrant children. These authors describe how the approach adopted in this high-performing elementary school enabled teachers and this school community to mitigate some of the effects of poverty. This case study helps document (a) potential instructional strategies, particularly those related to English language learners, that may be used to meet the academic needs of students; and (b) the social support system that might be accessed to provide social support systems for students and their families.

Kiersten Greene and Jean Anyon examine the ways in which poverty potentially limits educational achievement in "Urban School Reform, Family Support, and Student Achievement." Their article begins with an alarming description of the level of underachievement of low-income urban students in reading and math. These authors argue that although educational reforms fill classrooms with more books and supplies, provide teachers with professional development, and reduce class sizes, these changes alone may not be sufficient in terms of improving the academic achievement of low-income urban students. Greene and Anyon present research to build a case for providing increased financial and social supports to low-income urban families. These supports, they argue, are correlated with significant increases in reading and math achievement and may be part of the foundation for raising the educational achievement of poor students nationwide.

Lastly, in "The Short Supply of Saints: Limits on Replication of Models that 'Beat the Odds,'" Tamara Wilder and Rebecca Jacobsen examine the characteristics of teachers in the Knowledge Is Power Program (KIPP). KIPP is a chain of schools that are often cited as exemplar charter schools that "beat the odds." According to Wilder and Jacobsen, KIPP students' test scores are typically higher after just a few years compared to the scores of other Black and Hispanic urban students in regular public schools. Although previous research has examined the representativeness of students who attend KIPP schools, less attention has been paid to the teachers who are committed to doing "whatever it takes for students to learn." These authors argue that such models cannot practically be replicated on a large scale because few teachers are willing and/or able to make the time and financial commitment required of teachers in these model schools. They suggest that experts instead focus on building communities that beat the odds through a wide array of social and economic reforms that support children's health and social development.

REFERENCES

American Federation of Teachers. (1999). *Taking responsibility for ending social promotion: A guide for educators and state and local leaders.* Washington, DC: Author.

Berliner, D. C. (2005, August 2). Our impoverished view of educational reform. *TCRecord.* Retrieved from http://www.tcrecord.org/content.asp?contentid=1206

Bowman, B. (2002). Love to read: An introduction. In B. Bowman (Ed.), *Love to read: Essays in developing and enhancing early literacy skills of African American children* (pp. vii–ix). Washington, DC: National Black Child Development Institute.

Cavanagh, S. (2007, December 12). Poverty's effect on U.S. scores greater than for other nations. *Education Week, 27*(15), 1, 13.

Delgado-Gaitan, C. (1990). *Literacy for empowerment: The role of parents in children's education.* New York, NY: Falmer.

Duncan, G. J., & Magnuson, K. A. (2005). Can family socioeconomic resources account for racial and ethnic score gap? *The Future of Children, 15*(1), 35–54.

Gee, J. P. (1991). Socio-cultural approaches to literacy. *Annual Review of Applied Linguistics, 12,* 31–48.

Heath, B. (1983). *Ways with words: Language, life, and work in communities and classrooms.* Cambridge, England: Cambridge University Press.

Hoff, E. (2003). The specificity of environmental influence: Socioeconomic status affects early vocabulary development via maternal speech. *Child Development, 74,* 1368–1378.

Jencks, C., & Phillips, M. (1998). The black and white test score gap: An introduction. In C. Jencks & M. Phillips (Eds.), *The black and white test score gap* (pp. 1–51). Washington, DC: Brookings Institution.

Kellett, M., & Dar, A. (2007). *Children researching links between poverty and literacy.* York, England: Joseph Rowntree Foundation.

Lane, K. K., Gresham, F. M., & O'Shaughnessy, T. E. (2002). *Intervention for children with or at risk for emotional and behavioral disorders.* Boston, MA: Allyn & Bacon.

Lemke, M., Sen, A., Pahlke, E., Partelow, L., Miller, D., Williams, T., ... Jocelyn, L. (2005). *International outcomes of learning in mathematics literacy and problem solving: PISA 2003 results from the U.S. perspective.* Washington, DC: U.S. Department of Education, National Center for Education Statistics.

Machin, S., & McNally, S. (2006). *Education and child poverty. A literature review.* York, England: Joseph Rowntree Foundation.

National Commision on Excellence in Education. (1983, April). *A nation at risk: The imperative of educational reform. A report to the Nation and the Secretary of Education, United States Department of Education.* Washington, DC: U.S. Government Printing Office.

Rothstein, R. (2004). *Class and schools: Using social, economic and educational reform to close the black-white achievement gap.* Washington, DC: Economic Policy Institute.

Torgeson, J. (2000). Individual differences in response to early intervention in reading: The lingering problem of treatment resistance. *Learning Disabilities Research and Practice, 15,* 55–64.

Valdes, G. (1996). *Con respecto: Bridging the distance between culturally diverse families and school.* New York, NY: Teachers College Press.

Vygotsky, L. S. (1962). *Thought and language.* Cambridge, MA: MIT Press.

Vygotsky, L. S. (1978). *Mind in society: The development of higher psychological process.* (M. Cole, V. John-Streiner, S. Scribner, & E. Souberman, Trans.). Cambridge, MA: Harvard University Press.

Children and Adolescents From Poverty and Reading Development: A Research Review

ALPANA BHATTACHARYA

Queens College, City University of New York, Flushing, New York, USA

This article reviews the relationship between poverty and reading achievement in America's schools. It then discusses how to advance the reading proficiencies of students from economically impoverished homes. It gives particular emphasis to school–home partnerships and sociocultural literacy practices.

In her article "High-Poverty Schools That Beat the Odds," Cunningham (2006) stated that "poverty is the largest correlate of reading achievement" and "schools with large numbers of poor children seldom achieve their goals at the end-of-grade literacy tests" (p. 382). Similarly, Neuman (2006) reported that children from low-income families score on average 60% below children from higher income families, and once the children from poverty fall behind, they tend to stay behind.

Although explanations for this achievement gap are abounding, there are two primary and contrasting schools of thought. One view argues that children from poor families receive no or few valuable literacy experiences at home. The other view argues that children from poor homes receive varied literacy experiences from print-embedded activities, such as watching a character on television read a book, reading names from a comic book, and reading the cable TV listings. Children from poor families are also exposed to literacy experiences through daily life routines such as reading names on envelopes, reading the information on coupons before going to the grocery store, and reading a label in a shirt (Purcell-Gates, L'Allier, & Smith, 1995).

The first view tends to blame the children and their families for the children's academic difficulties (Compton-Lilly, 2000). The second view upholds literacy as social practices (Landis & Moje, 2003). In other words, children's uses of written language during everyday life—their outside-of-school literacy experiences—are taken into account to understand their struggles with reading and writing and to support their struggles with literacy instruction.

To help experts understand the validity of these views and what can be done to teach poor children to read effectively, this article reviews the literature (a) describing the home literacy experiences of children from poverty and (b) demonstrating the effectiveness of literacy practices with such children.

HOME ENVIRONMENT AND READING ACHIEVEMENT

Home environment, which includes family income, educational resources, and parental involvement, plays an essential role in the academic achievement of students in Grades K–12. In recent years, its influence on reading achievement has received considerable attention (e.g., Molfese, Modglin, & Molfese, 2003; Molfese & Molfese, 2002; Parcel & Dufur, 2001; Rashid, Morris, & Sevcik, 2005). Researchers have suggested a strong relationship between school-age children's home environments and academic achievement, particularly reading abilities (Molfese et al., 2003). Parents who provide age-appropriate, cognitively stimulating home environments (e.g., provide books, computers, and musical instruments) and who involve themselves in their children's education (e.g., discuss school-related issues) tend to strengthen children's reading achievement (Eamon, 2005; Parcel & Dufur, 2001).

Molfese et al. (2003) examined the relationship between home environment and children's reading abilities by classifying home environment measures into proximal and distal measures. The researchers classified family income, parental occupation, and parental education as distal measures because of their indirect impact on children. They classified educational resources, parental involvement, and parenting practices as proximal measures because these measures exert a direct influence on children. Both distal and proximal measures were found to be related to the reading ability of children, but the proximal measures were more strongly related to reading ability during the early childhood years than the middle childhood years. Differences in the relationship of the environmental measures and reading ability were also found between successful readers and poor readers. Although there was some relationship between the environmental measures and the reading abilities of poor readers, the strength of the relationship was primarily nonsignificant for both the distal and proximal measures during the middle childhood years and weak for the proximal measures during the early childhood years. The researchers concluded that home environment plays an important role in the reading development of children, but variables other than proximal and distal measures, such as short-term memory, processing speed, and auditory processing, should be considered in trying to understand the reading development of children.

Parcel and Dufur (2001) also investigated the effects of home environment on children's reading achievement. Specifically, they examined the relationship of reading achievement to three kinds of capital at home: family social capital, family human capital, and family financial capital. Family social capital referred to the home's physical environment, its cognitive stimulation, and the parents' affect and disciplinary style. Family human capital involved parental education, marital status, and mental ability. Family financial capital included parental income and material resources. The researchers found that family social capital was strongly related to children's reading achievement. For children of elementary and middle school age, higher levels of family social capital were associated with increased levels of reading achievement. For example, children from smaller intact families, in which both parents were educated, were financially secure, were committed to each other, and had reasonable work schedules, tended to have higher levels of reading achievement than children from families in which the social capital was diluted because of higher maternal work hours or more siblings in the household. The researchers attributed the higher levels of achievement to two factors: the higher allocations of time and resources parents gave their children.

Rashid et al. (2005) investigated how the home literacy environment influenced the reading achievement of 65 children with reading disabilities. Rashid and her colleagues defined *home literacy environment* as "participation in literacy-related activities in the home" (p. 2). It generally included features such as the availability of print material and frequency of reading. The researchers gathered information about parents' and children's individual and shared reading and nonreading activities. Results showed that the direct relationship between home literacy environment and reading achievement was not as strong as the researchers had expected. In fact, children's home literacy activities were not related to their reading abilities. More specifically, data indicated that even when reading materials and literacy activities were available in the home, a large percentage of the children did not engage in reading activities and spent several hours participating in nonreading activities such as watching entertainment television. The researchers hypothesized that the weak relationship between children's home literacy environment and reading achievement might stem from (a) limited independent reading experiences of the children, (b) below-average cognitive abilities of the children, (c) less joint reading between parents and children at home, and (d) parents' difficulties with reading. In other words, children's reading difficulties may be a barrier to reading activities in an otherwise enriched literacy environment.

In sum, children's reading achievement is positively related to the educational resources in homes and to parents who provide quality time and attention and cognitively stimulating activities. Furthermore, educated parents with fewer children, higher paying jobs, and reasonable work hours can better support their children's academic achievement. Reading disabilities, however, weaken the strength of these relationships.

PSYCHOSOCIAL PERSPECTIVE: POVERTY AND READING ACHIEVEMENT

Encouraged by findings supporting the relationship between home environment and children's reading achievement, researchers have examined the relationship between poverty and reading achievement (e.g., Bradley, Corwyn, McAdoo, & Coll, 2001; Dubow & Ippolito, 1994; Eamon, 2002, 2005; Guo, 1998; Nievar & Luster, 2006). Specifically, studies have examined mother's education, mother's age at child's birth, the number of children in the home, and mother's marital status (Bradley et al., 2001; Dubow & Ippolito, 1994; Eamon, 2002, 2005; Guo, 1998).

Dubow and Ippolito (1994) assessed the effects of prior poverty and recent poverty on the reading achievement of children ages 5 through 8. Prior poverty was a family's poverty status 4 years before the first reading assessment. Recent poverty was poverty within 4 years of the first and last reading assessments. The quality of the home environment was assessed with the Home Observation for Measurement of the Environment scale, which examined the home's physical environment, emotional support, cognitive activities, and cognitive stimulation. The researchers found that poverty during the child's preschool years significantly predicted the child's academic achievement in elementary school. In other words, when preschool children from high-poverty homes later attended elementary school, their reading achievement was poor irrespective of mother's education, mother's age at child's birth, the presence of a spouse in the home, and the number of children in the home.

In interpreting these findings, Dubow and Ippolito cautioned readers not to ignore other factors that might influence children's reading achievement. They explained that their study might have masked these factors, as poverty inhibits the ability of parents to provide cognitively stimulating and emotionally supportive homes. They hypothesized that cognitively stimulating and emotionally supportive homes can increase reading achievement independent of parents' childbirth age, marital status, or education or the number of children in the home.

Bradley et al. (2001) investigated the relative effects of ethnicity and poverty status on children's and adolescents' home environments. Home environment measures included mother's education, family income, parental responsiveness (e.g., answering child's questions, conversing with the child, hugging and praising the child), learning stimulation (e.g., providing musical instruments, purchasing books, arranging trips to a museum), and other activities (e.g., doing routine chores, managing own time, eating meals with parents). Bradley and his colleagues reported statistically significant differences between poor and nonpoor families across African American, Euro-American, and Hispanic American families. With minor differences among the groups, poverty proportionally decreased the availability of developmentally enriching materials and experiences in homes.

Eamon (2002) studied the effects of poverty on the reading achievement of adolescents aged 12 through 14. She hypothesized that poverty would be correlated with reading achievement because of constraints on parents' ability to provide cognitively stimulating and emotionally supportive homes. As a part of her conceptual mediation model of poverty and reading achievement, she considered mother's education, mother's age at child's birth, the number of parents in the home, and the number of children in the home. She found that poverty was indirectly associated with reading achievement through its connection with cognitive stimulation and emotional support at home. Adolescents from high-poverty backgrounds tended to have lower reading scores; their homes provided few cognitively stimulating activities and materials and less emotional support. She concluded that economic hardships produced stress and depression, limiting the parents' ability to provide cognitive stimulation and emotional support. This in turn lowered adolescents' reading achievement.

Investigations of the psychosocial processes within low-income families have indicated that parental involvement in children's school activities is related to parental income and education. Generally, researchers found that parents from low-income communities were uninvolved in their children's school lives: Parents were inattentive to homework, they infrequently attended school functions, and they sparingly volunteered for school activities (Evans, 2004). Parents with lower levels of education were also reported as being less likely to interact positively with their children (Nievar & Luster, 2006), monitor their children's school experiences, or encourage their children's engagement with literary (Evans, 2004). This research, however, presents a limited view of the impact of poverty on children. This is because the adverse physical conditions that poor children and families face coexist with suboptimal psychosocial conditions. To more reliably and accurately identify the relation between the home environment and the academic achievement of poor children requires a cumulative investigation of the psychosocial and physical environmental factors that influence their lives (Evans, 2004).

Among the in-home variables that influence the reading achievement of children and adolescents from poverty are the availability of cognitive stimulation and emotional support (Eamon, 2002, 2005; McLoyd, 1998; Nievar & Luster, 2006). Parental stress from inadequate economic resources has been identified as adversely affecting the intent of poor parents to provide cognitive stimulation for their children. Less cognitive stimulation, in turn, is associated with lower reading ability (Eamon, 2005; Nievar & Luster, 2006). Although home factors—such as educational toys and games, family activities and conversational skills, and parental encouragement and assistance for academic skills—are strongly related to the development of reading ability (Eamon, 2005; Molfese & Molfese, 2002), literacy opportunities available to children within the home environment need not be fancy or extraordinary (Molfese & Molfese, 2002). In other words, "family income positively affects child outcomes not so much for what it can buy, but for what it represents" (McLoyd, 1998, p. 193). It is the quality and quantity of child-centered activities in the home rather than the socioeconomic status of the family that influences reading abilities (Molfese & Molfese, 2002; Share, Jorm, Maclean, Matthews, & Waterman, 1983).

Differences in children's cognitive development and school achievement are generally attributed to family income. In addition, persistent poverty more adversely affects children's cognitive abilities and educational achievement than occasional poverty. Poverty experienced during early childhood has been reported to have far more detrimental effects on academic achievement than poverty experienced during middle childhood and adolescence (McLoyd, 1998). Research has also found that the longer children and adolescents lived in poverty, the less likely they were to be exposed to cognitively stimulating and emotionally supportive homes (Eamon, 2005; Evans, 2004). This in turn has been predictive of lower reading achievement (Eamon, 2005).

Long-term poverty exerts substantial influences on children and adolescents, but the time patterns of these influences differ. As a result, the influences of persistent poverty have been classified into early family influences and late family influences. Early influences focus on the critical period of childhood ranging from birth through early adolescence. Late influences of poverty target early adolescence. Poverty experienced in childhood appears to influence cognitive ability (i.e., rate of learning), whereas poverty experienced in early adolescence seems to influence cognitive achievement (i.e., what is learned). These conclusions are consistent with the view that childhood is a crucial period for the development of cognitive ability, whereas early adolescence is particularly important for achievement. Poverty has a larger effect on childhood ability than adolescence ability because ability is a stable individual trait and tends to be determined by environmental and genetic factors early in life. In contrast, poverty has a more substantial influence on achievement during early adolescence than during childhood because achievement represents acquired skills and is a product of environmental and social interactions (Guo, 1998).

SOCIOCULTURAL PERSPECTIVE: POVERTY AND READING ACHIEVEMENT

Many people in the public believe that parents from high-poverty urban households are uninterested, uncaring, and incompetent and that they do not have the necessary academic or parenting skills to address the academic difficulties of their children (Compton-Lilly, 2000; Purcell-Gates et al., 1995). This view has been challenged by ethnographic research (e.g., Compton-Lilly, 2000; Cunningham, 2006; Moll, Amanti, Neff, & Gonzalez, 1992; Purcell-Gates, 1996; Purcell-Gates et al., 1995).

Compton-Lilly (2000), for example, explored the concept of reading held by poor inner city parents and their first-grade children. She interviewed 10 first-grade students and their parents over 9 months. Interview data suggested that urban parents and their children placed a high value on reading and that they expected teachers to have high expectations for their students. Parents also expressed the need to monitor their children and to intervene when their children displayed unacceptable behavior, academic progress, and attitude at home and at school. Contrary to the prevalent negative stereotype, Compton-Lilly found that urban parents from poverty were concerned about and actively involved in educating their children. Parents tried to achieve this balance by holding high expectations for their children and developing a caring relationship with them.

Purcell-Gates et al. (1995) explored the general notion that children from low-income inner city families experience no or very few literacy events in their homes and thus are less ready to learn. Over 2 to 3 months, Purcell-Gates and her colleagues observed and recorded the use of print in the daily lives of 24 poor inner city children 4 to 6 years of age and their families. The researchers noted all uses of print (e.g., reading storybooks, reading recipes, writing shopping lists, writing letters) and the presence of all literacy materials (e.g., dictionaries, magazines, Bibles, novels) in the homes. Although all families were similar in terms of socioeconomic status, they differed in terms of their literacy practices. High-literacy families used print for varied types of activities such as daily routines, entertainment, school, interpersonal communication, and religion; in contrast, low-literacy families used print mainly for daily routines and entertainment. Results indicated vast variations in the number and types of print used in high-poverty families. Whereas some children had numerous literacy experiences, others had fewer literacy opportunities, which could have adversely affected their ability to read. This study suggested that deficiencies in family literacy practices rather than poverty seemed to adversely affect the children's literacy development.

Purcell-Gates (1996) extended her exploration of the relationship between home literacy experiences and the reading achievement of young children from low-income families by analyzing data related to in-home uses of print and examining young children's knowledge of written language. In a year-long descriptive study, Purcell-Gates conducted in-home observations of 20 low-income families, including 24 children 4 to 6 years old. The literacy levels of parents ranged from low literate (i.e., could not read or write well enough to participate in their daily social lives or workplaces) to functionally literate (i.e., could read and write to transact in daily affairs and within a job). The low socioeconomic status of the families was established through self-report, residence in public housing projects, qualification for Aid to Families with Dependent Children payments, and qualification of children for Head Start or free lunch. All families spoke English at home and were from varied ethnic and racial groups. The relationship between the use of print in the home, children's knowledge of written language, and reading achievement was determined through the analysis of different factors. Factors included parental literacy level, home literacy involvement (e.g., mother, father, cousin, and friend involved in literacy activities with the focal child), child's educational level, literacy events (e.g., reading, writing, and drawing activities), social domains (e.g., types of reading and writing activities), text levels (e.g., complexity of print being read), and written knowledge tasks.

Results of the Purcell-Gates (1996) investigation focused on three areas: (a) social domains mediated by print, (b) text levels across families, and (c) children's knowledge of written language. Results for the social domains showed that the low-income families used print mainly for "entertainment" (e.g., reading magazines or television guides) and "daily living routines" (e.g., reading cooking recipes or food ingredients). Analysis of text levels revealed that low-income families' print reading involved word and sentences. Low-income families were reading words and single sentences (e.g., ingredients printed on cereal boxes) as a part of their daily living routines and entertainment. Regarding children's knowledge of written language, Purcell-Gates found that although most children understood that print is meaningful, that print maps onto speech, and that print is different from speech, they had not grasped the ways in which print functions and the fact that print involves the linear arrangement of letters.

Purcell-Gates's (1996) data analysis identified three patterns of home literacy and children's knowledge of written language. First, children from low-income households that had greater exposure to print and greater mother–child literacy interactions learned the nature and forms of written language more compared to children from families with low use of print and mother–child interactions. Second, children from low-income homes in which parents read more complex text, both for their own purposes and their children's sake, demonstrated more advanced understanding of the nature and forms of written language. Third, parents from low-income households, irrespective of their literacy level, began or increased their involvement in literacy learning (e.g., teaching letters and words, reading to their children) at the start of their children's formal literacy instruction in school.

Moll et al. (1992) conducted a qualitative study of working-class families from Mexican communities in Arizona. Ten teachers participated in the study. Each teacher conducted ethnographic observations and interviews of three households of students from his or her classroom. A total of 100 observations and interviews were conducted in 25 households. The ethnographic study provided teachers with opportunities to learn about their students and their families and to develop a positive view of working-class households as containing cultural and cognitive resources that could be used in classroom instruction. The observation and interview data contradicted the common notion that working-class families are disorganized socially and deficient intellectually. In contrast to prevalent stereotypes, Moll's team found that the working-class parents not only cared for their children but also were supportive of their education. When given the opportunity, the parents served as a cognitive resource by sharing their knowledge of work with the teachers and their students.

Through classroom observation, interviews, and a survey, Cunningham (2006) obtained data from six schools that demonstrated that schools with large numbers of poor children can obtain high levels of literacy. Of the 12 factors that Cunningham identified as important for high literacy achievement—assessment, community involvement, comprehensive curriculum, student engagement, instruction, leadership, materials, parent participation, perseverance and persistence, professional development, real reading and writing, and specialist support—the six schools ranked high on only two factors: student engagement and real reading and writing. Each of the six schools had done better than expected on the state literacy tests because of extremely high levels of student engagement with literacy activities. Students also spent a lot of time actually reading during guided reading and self-selected reading time and during an after-school program. Although ranked as less important than student engagement and real reading and writing, parent participation in literacy activities also contributed to the students' high literacy achievement. Parents participated in monthly sessions that focused on helping children with homework and computers. Cunningham's study shows that high-poverty schools can achieve high levels of literacy through student engagement and parent participation in literacy activities.

Collectively, the qualitative studies described in this section shed light on the relationship between home literacy experiences and the reading achievement of children from poor households. In particular, the studies inform readers of the ways in which parents do or do not participate in their children's literacy acquisition (Purcell-Gates, 1996). The studies suggest that the lower reading achievement of poor children is often due not to household poverty per se but to a paucity of in-home literacy experiences. This challenges the belief that all children from poverty have little ability to learn and will inevitably achieve little (Purcell-Gates et al., 1995). Children from poor households that provide them with good literacy experiences will likely achieve much more than their peers who have a paucity of quality literacy experiences.

IDENTITY AND READING

As Compton-Lilly (2006) asserted, "Children's personal histories as readers, their past successes, the official criteria for determining reading competence, and their current struggles all contribute to the ways in which children identify themselves as readers" (p. 59). In other words, children's and adolescents' identities as readers are formed and shaped through their interactions in and out of school. Furthermore, their identities as readers reflect the meaning they derive from their texts and from their social position in and out of school (Moje, 2002; Moje, Dillon, & O'Brien, 2000). Because identities are formed from relationships with teachers and with other students and are influenced by readers' social positions (Compton-Lilly, 2006; McCarthey & Moje, 2002), these social relationships influence children's development as readers (Christian & Bloome, 2004).

One aspect of classrooms that influences students' identities as readers is their language. All students enter their classrooms equipped with the language and culture of their home and community. Some students' cultural resources match the school's expectations and values related to reading; other students' do not (Christian & Bloome, 2004; Compton-Lilly, 2006). A congruent match tends to advance students' identity and reading development. This is because congruence helps students earn a commendable social position, reaffirming their identity. Conversely, a mismatch can create a social disadvantage, prompting the mismatched students to shun their culture, language, and identity and adopt those of the dominant society (Christian & Bloome, 2004).

Besides language, identity construction also involves values and practices established within a classroom. Whereas some students find classroom reading and writing tasks enjoyable and socially enhancing, others find the same tasks unpleasant and socially destructive. Students in the lower reading groups, for example, are often viewed as lacking the ability to become better readers. Their lower level performance on reading and writing tasks relegates them to lower social positions in their classrooms, which become part of their social and reading identities. This strongly suggests that differential achievement between good and poor readers is unlikely to be eliminated only through instruction that focuses on skills and abilities. A complementary focus is needed, one that strengthens the close connection between students' social identities and their development as readers and writers (Christian & Bloome, 2004). In other words, teachers and students should create a supportive learning community within which students can develop their identities as learners, readers, and writers of text and optimize their understanding of text through dialogue, apprenticeship, and mentoring (Bernhard et al., 2006). As a part of their literacy instruction, teachers can give students opportunities to examine the construction of their identities as mediated by their culture and social relations. One way to help students explore their identities as readers is to engage them in explicit discussions about how they see themselves relative to the texts they are reading (McCarthey & Moje, 2002). Discussions of texts give students the opportunity not only to talk about their own lives and interests but to reflect on their identities in a positive manner and develop an affective bond to literacy. Furthermore, discussions of texts offer students the opportunity to take pride in themselves and their families (Bernhard et al., 2006). Finally, discussions of text also help students to connect knowledge of literacy from home with the genre within their school (Duke & Purcell-Gates, 2003).

Literacy instruction in the United States is often derived from European cultural and social practices. Literacy instruction founded in European culture and practices tends to privilege and support the identity and literacy learning of students from these cultures (Moje, Dillon, & O'Brien, 2000). So that students from minority cultures are not disadvantaged by this, each child's positive attributes and uniqueness should be stressed. Teachers can do this by providing all students with opportunities to recognize their similarities and differences (Christian & Bloome, 2004). More specifically, teachers can provide students with opportunities to read and discuss texts about different cultures. This can help students understand the values, beliefs, practices, and communication styles of different cultural groups (McCarthey & Moje, 2002). This can also provide students with opportunities and tools for learning to read while learning to appreciate one another (Christian & Bloome, 2004). Such readings and discussions may help to counter the marginalization that often emanates from age, race, class, ethnicity, gender, ability, language, religion, and sexual orientation (Moje et al., 2000).

FACILITATING THE READING DEVELOPMENT OF STUDENTS FROM POVERTY

The No Child Left Behind Act of 2002 requires schools to educate all students effectively, including students at risk for failure, those with disabilities, those with limited English proficiency, and those from low-income and ethnic minority backgrounds (Conley & Hinchman, 2004). By focusing on two important areas—school–home partnerships and sociocultural literacy practices—schools may well accelerate the reading achievement of students from poverty. What follows is a discussion of both recommendations.

School–Home Partnerships and Reading Development

Parental involvement is positively associated with children's reading development and educational achievement (Darling, 2008; Ordonez-Jasis, & Ortis, 2006; Powell-Smith, Shinn, Stoner, & Good, 2000). Increased family involvement in school is associated with increased literacy performance, particularly among children in low-income families (Dearing, Kreider, Simpkins, & Weiss, 2006). Thus, many family literacy professionals view parents as the first and most important teachers of children's reading acquisition (Breitborde & Swiniarski, 2002; Edwards, 1992; Padak & Rasinski, 2007).

Although the link between parental involvement and reading achievement is vital (Dearing et al., 2006; Ediger, 2008) and parents play a critical role in the literacy development of their children (Baker, 2003; Morrow, Kuhn, & Schwanenflugel, 2006), parents' involvement in reading development need not be complex or time consuming (Padak & Rasinski, 2007). Parental involvement in children's reading development can be as simple as modeling literate behaviors, answering children's questions, and helping with homework (Dearing et al., 2006; Padak & Rasinski, 2007).

PROVIDING FAMILY LITERACY EDUCATION

Richardson, Miller, Richardson, and Sacks (2008) claimed, "Most parents want their children to be successful readers but some parents are not confident in how to provide information, or using strategies and activities to promote reading success" (p. 3). Despite research support for the value of family reading activities and parents talking with their children, advising parents to read to their children or to encourage their children to read aloud may not be enough. Parents may need specific guidelines and suggestions for participating in the reading development of their children (Padak & Rasinski, 2007; Scales & Snyder, 2004). A major cause of the academic under-preparedness of poor children is likely the harsh social and economic circumstances that limit parents' ability to meet the day-to-day demands of family life. Thus, no single educational intervention will likely overcome the disadvantages faced by young children from poor families. Planning and applying educational interventions will require paying attention to the needs and resources of individual families (Huebner, 2000). Experts will have to answer the following question: How can we help families overcome the harsh realities that are impeding their children's educational progress? Following are descriptions of four projects that help to answer this question.

PARENTS AS PARTNERS IN READING

Rather than blaming poor parents for their children's school failure, Edwards (1992) designed a book-reading program, Parents as Partners in Reading, to teach parents how to book-read with their children. The program provides parents with opportunities to observe their children at school in reading groups. In addition, teachers at a family learning center provide parents with instruction and materials for book reading with their children at home. The book-reading program consists of 23 sessions of 2 hr each divided into four phases: coaching, peer modeling, guided practice, and parent–child interactions.

In the coaching phase, teachers model effective book-reading strategies with children; teachers discuss the modeled strategies with parents; and parents watch videos of book-reading strategies, such as pointing to and describing pictures. In the peer-modeling phase, parents role-play and model effective book-reading strategies with their peers. In guided practice, teachers give parents corrective feedback and praise. Finally, in the parent–child interactions phase, parents share books with their children and implement the book-reading strategies they have learned.

According to Edwards (1992), Parents as Partners in Reading helped parents facilitate their children's development as readers. The program taught parents how to share books with their children, what to expect of their children in school, and what their children could do with appropriate parental guidance. In addition, the program enabled parents to help their children with school activities and increased parents' confidence in their own reading abilities.

BRIDGES TO LITERACY

Waldbart, Meyers, and Meyers's (2006) Bridges to Literacy program fosters the reading development of poor children by forging a connection between schools and poor families. The Bridges to Literacy project works to increase parent–child literacy interactions and to promote school–family collaboration in reading development. The project has three phases. Phase 1 is school–family collaboration. This involves poor parents participating in focus group discussions with an elementary school principal and university personnel. The focus group gives parents an opportunity to share their concerns and interests about their children's literacy development and to consider strategies for carrying out at-home reading activities. Parents then participate in two in-class demonstrations of shared-reading instruction conducted by the teacher with the whole class. This is followed by a question-and-answer session about the demonstrations. Phase 1 also involves a lending library, from which the teacher checks out books for the students and supplements them with assignments for home. The assignments are designed to support the parents' use of the strategies that were modeled in the demonstrations (Waldbart et al., 2006).

Phase 2 is also school–family collaboration. Similar to Phase 1, it consists of a focus group, in-class modeling, questions and answers, and the lending library. As opposed to the whole-class instruction of Phase 1, Phase 2 emphasizes small-group, teacher-led guided reading, and individual reading conferences. These demonstrations are conducted after school. Phase 2 adds two features: a tip sheet for parents for at-home reading, and two home visits in which staff model shared-reading techniques. The tip sheet reinforces the parents' use of strategies for the at-home reading of the books borrowed by their children. The home visits involve three forms of shared reading. A Bridges staff member first models a shared-reading technique with the child, using the tip sheet as a reference. Then the parent reads the book with the child and gets feedback from the staff member. Finally, the parent independently reads a book with the child, using the shared-reading strategies included in the tip sheet (Waldbart et al., 2006).

During Phase 3, three home visits of 45 min are conducted about 2 weeks apart. The visits focus on modeling paired reading and conducting a semistructured interview. A Bridges staff member first models paired reading and discusses the strategy with the parent. Then the parent and child engage in paired reading and discuss the process. Finally, the staff member engages the child in literacy-related assignments, such as drawing a picture about a favorite part of a book. The interview elicits information about the home literacy environment and enables the participants to discuss how to improve it (Waldbart et al., 2006).

The findings of the Bridges to Literacy program (Waldbart et al., 2006) challenge the popular view that parents from poor neighborhoods have low expectations for their children's literacy and that they refuse to be involved in their children's schooling. From their findings, Waldbart and her colleagues concluded that family involvement at schools could be increased through a focus on families as architects of intervention. Including families in the design and implementation of academic interventions can help families recognize their own expertise in facilitating reading development. Waldbart and colleagues' work makes a compelling argument for their recommendations.

FAMILY FLUENCY PROGRAM

Morrow et al. (2006) believe that to work, home–school programs not only need to invite parents to participate in their children's schooling, but also need to involve parents in reading activities that are easy to use, fun, and nonthreatening. Consequently, the researchers developed the Family Fluency Program, a program of reading activities that are easy to understand and begin, take little time, and help parents see quick progress in their children's reading.

The Family Fluency Program (Morrow et al., 2006) tries to involve parents in literacy activities at home and to heighten their awareness of oral reading strategies. It does this through a two-pronged approach. One prong sends home basal readers twice weekly for parent–child reading. Parents are asked to document their joint book-reading behaviors with their children and to talk about their children's interactions with them during the joint-reading activities. The other prong involves three workshops to heighten parents' awareness of reading strategies to enhance children's reading fluency. The workshops demonstrate echo reading, choral reading, and partner reading strategies and discuss the importance of oral reading concepts such as decoding words, learning new vocabulary, and using intonation to express correctly the meaning of the text. Parents are given handouts, audiotapes, and videos that explain and demonstrate the strategies. They are also given opportunities to practice echo reading, choral reading, and partner reading with the researchers, children, and other parents.

The Family Fluency Program increased parents' literacy involvement with their children at home, parents' use of fluency-building activities at home, and parents' awareness of the importance of fluency training in reading development. Parents reported reading to or with their children and helping their children with homework three to five times every week. Parents used choral reading, partner reading, and pacing as strategies for building the reading fluency of children at home (Morrow et al., 2006).

DIALOGIC READING

Like the previously described programs, Huebner's (2000) Dialogic Reading was designed to increase the at-home reading that poor parents do with their children. Dialogic Reading attempts to strengthen the expressive language and reading abilities of children from poor homes through parent questions, expansion of child's responses, parent–child reading activities, and parental praise of children's telling and retelling of stories. To do this, Huebner provides two 1-hr parent training sessions that use video illustrations, modeling, role play, and discussions. To guide their children's oral participation during book reading, parents are taught to use "what," "where," and "why" questions, open-ended questions, corrective feedback, and praise. Parents are given a summary of goals for children's at-home reading, reminder sheets to use during at-home reading, and reading logs to keep track of reading.

Like the previously discussed programs, Dialogic Reading proved successful. It increased the frequency of at-home reading and heightened parents' perceptions of their children's enjoyment of shared reading. It also forged a link between the question-and-answer language of formal schooling and the interactive discourse patterns of the home via parent questions, child responses, and parent–child discussions of shared readings.

To summarize, home–school partnerships in literacy education offer ongoing training to parents and regularly scheduled home visits to help them use the training. These programs have demonstrated that involving families in shared-reading activities at home improves children's reading abilities and achievement.

SUPPLEMENTING HOME LITERACY RESOURCES

Although many parents support their children's school achievement by attending parent workshops, accompanying their children on class trips, and performing school-related tasks at home, some parents cannot do these things. They lack the time and resources (Dever & Burts, 2002). For example, they may have to work two jobs to pay the rent and feed their children. They may not have the money for bus fare. They may be poorly educated and thus unable to help their children with homework. One way to help these parents strengthen their children's reading is to provide these parents with resources, information, and ideas for reading at home (Richardson et al., 2008).

One model of providing poor parents with resources is the Family Literacy Bags project (Dever & Burts, 2002). This model has many variations: Backpacking Partnership (Richgels & Wold, 1998), Bilingual Bags (Avery, 2003), Gator Bag (Hall, 2007), and Luggage and Baggage (Grande, 2004). The model and its variations promote family involvement in children's reading. Families are provided with educational information and materials (e.g., books, games, flashcards, art supplies, activity sheets, and response journals) to use in working with their children at home (Dever & Burts, 2002; Richardson et al., 2008). Although each variation of literacy bags may serve a different purpose, the major goal is the same: to motivate children and their families to read together, enjoy books, and discuss their joint book-reading activities (Richardson et al., 2008).

The Family Literacy Bags project has increased parental involvement in book reading and related activities as well as sustained interest and enthusiasm in children's use of literacy materials and activities at home. Schools have a relatively simple way of promoting literacy by sending home literacy bags of high-quality books of varying reading levels and genres, extension activities focused around a theme (e.g., gardening, pets, food), materials for extension activities, and a guidebook to help parents read books to their children (Dever & Burts, 2002).

The Dog Gone Good Reading Program illustrates another way to supplement home literacy resources and enhance students' home reading experiences (Koskinen et al., 1999). The program emphasizes shared reading and repeated reading in class and home, using emergent literacy and first-grade books.

After participating in small-group guided reading (e.g., children look at a book's cover and predict what will happen in the story) and shared reading (e.g., the teacher orally reads a book to the students; the teacher and students then orally reread it together), students take a book home to read it two or three times independently or to someone. An inexpensive backpack with the logo of a dog and the title "Dog Gone Good Reading" is given to each student for carrying books to and from school. A Dog Gone Good Reading checkout chart containing library card pockets with each student's name is used to manage the daily book exchange. To foster motivation, language expression, and school–home communication, students share their home reading experiences in the class. Parents are told about the program during parent conferences and are encouraged to participate as listeners who help their child when needed (Koskinen et al., 1999).

In analyzing the results of their initial study, Koskinen and her colleagues (1999) found that the rereading strategy helped students gain information and handle difficult texts. The program facilitated the shared rereading of books between parents and their children and helped students feel successful. It made literacy a pleasurable learning activity within the home. Teachers and parents believed it improved students' literacy achievement.

Like Koskinen and her colleagues (1999), Padak and Rasinski (2007) have also advocated that schools provide books for reading at home. They challenged the view that parents should stop reading aloud to their children when children begin to read independently. Instead, Padak and Rasinski suggested that parents read age-appropriate articles or book chapters to their children, listen to their children read school books, read alternative paragraphs or pages with their children, read near their children while they read materials of their own, and encourage their children to read aloud to a family pet or stuffed animal.

Supporting Low-Literate and Illiterate Parents

As discussed earlier, support for reading is associated with the availability of reading materials in the home and the frequency with which parents read to their children. Unfortunately, many high-poverty parents are poor readers (Baker, 2003). Thus, they may not feel adequate to help their children develop literacy abilities, to participate in school activities, or to discuss their children's learning problems with teachers (Smith & Elish-Piper, 2002). They may avoid these situations. Unknowingly, they may perpetuate illiteracy by failing to provide their children with the resources and activities needed to foster literacy. Cooter (2006) calls this *intergenerational illiteracy*, "a socio-cultural phenomenon whereby illiterate parents inadvertently sponsor home conditions that may seriously hinder their children's reading and writing development, thus perpetuating a cycle of illiteracy" (p. 698). Not surprisingly, intergenerational illiteracy often exists in high-poverty urban and rural settings in which three or more generations of a family have poor literacy skills.

Given the illiteracy of many parents from high-poverty neighborhoods and their consequent hesitance to help their children with schoolwork, to involve themselves in school activities, and to communicate with their children's teachers (Cooter, 2006; Smith & Elish-Piper, 2002), schools need to address intergenerational illiteracy (Baker, 2003). Besides the pressing morality of doing so, schools that serve high-poverty communities need to address this illiteracy for legal reasons. Under the Improving America's Schools Act of 1994 and the Literacy Involves Families Together Act of 2000, schools receiving Title I funds must emphasize family literacy and parent involvement (Smith & Elish-Piper, 2002).

According to Cooter (2006), proactive teachers can help illiterate parents from low-income urban settings foster their children's reading development. More specifically, Cooter suggested three evidence-based strategies: talk and play; make-believe-alouds; and magazines, comics, and catalogs. *Talk and play* asks parents to set aside time to talk to their children while they both use toys. *Make-believe-alouds* help parents construct stories about pictures in a book and retell them to their children. The *magazines, comics, and catalogs* strategy encourages parents to show pictures found in reading materials and discuss them with their children. All three strategies can stimulate children's vocabulary and language abilities. Like Cooter, Padak and Rasinski (2006, 2007) asserted that parents can encourage their children's at-home reading by using household literacy materials, such as newspapers, shopping lists, and street signs. Parents can also help children watch and read the captioning on television shows.

Sociocultural Literacy Practices and Reading Development

Conventional literacy practices attribute poor students' reading problems to low language ability and inadequate home environment (Landis & Moje, 2003). Sociocultural literacy practices, in contrast, capitalize on poor students' diverse literacy experiences, language practices, and personal interests to promote literacy learning (Compton-Lilly, 2007). According to Moje, Overby, Tysvaer, and Morris (2008), the prevailing beliefs that poor students are unmotivated, that their reading is below the basic range, and that they shun reading outside of school are wrong. Students from poor neighborhoods do read. They frequently read Web sites, letters and notes, music lyrics, e-mails, magazines, novels, short stories, and plays. Generally, poor students read to obtain access to social networks and relationships, to seek models for self-improvement, and to get information about certain kinds of people. They also read to obtain facts, to prepare for college, and to follow news stories. Teachers therefore need to look closely at why poor students read and offer them lessons that build on and extend their habits and concerns. The problem may not be that poor students are unmotivated to read but that they are motivated by specific kinds of reading. In addition, the reading achievement of students from poor neighborhoods can be improved by bridging the gap between school and home experiences.

Smith and Elish-Piper (2002) have made numerous suggestions for bridging this gap. For example, students could interview family members about their hobbies and interests and then share their findings in class; they could supplement oral reports with family artifacts, scrapbooks, and video clips; they could take home books and share them with family members; they could invite family members to share their interests with the class. Teachers could take classes on a literacy walk. Younger students could identify letters, numbers, colors, words, and signs. Older students could write down words and phrases to study in class. Teachers could develop language lessons with the language students see on billboards and signs.

Like Smith and Elish-Piper (2002), Duke, Purcell-Gates, Hall, and Tower (2006) have identified numerous classroom activities that build on students' family and community experiences. As their activities "replicate or reflect reading and writing activities that occur in the lives of people outside of a learning-to-read-and-write context and purpose" (p. 346), Duke et al. call them *authentic literacy activities*. Examples include (a) literacy in response to community need and (b) literacy as a part of problem solving. One community-based literacy activity involved students reading about pond life and publishing a brochure answering questions about pond life. A problem-based literacy task involved students reading about simple machines (e.g., lever and pulleys) and writing procedural text on the removal of file cabinets from the classroom. Student-generated texts were placed in the classroom library and at a nature center.

The sociocultural perspective asserts that the reading achievement of students from poverty might also be strengthened by activities that stress different forms of materials or genres that students typically encounter. These include charts, poems, graphs, diagrams, pamphlets, brochures, advertisements, coupons, and students' personal drawings. Teachers could ask students to bring in materials from home, such as recipes, catalogs, applications, and announcements. Teachers could use these materials—from home and from the school—to develop reading activities. For example, reading instruction might stress the connections between the health curriculum and the food served at home. Teachers might link recipes, cookbooks, brochures, coupons, and advertisements to the food pyramid, exercise logs, and food group charts (Smith & Elish-Piper, 2002).

Reading instruction that attempts to bridge the gap between school and home might also stress the kinds of reading materials students are likely to see in their homes or neighborhoods. Thus, schools should take advantage of one ubiquitous reading material found in most poor neighborhoods: comic strips. Because comic strips are text structure with a story, and readers have to blend the print and the graphics to comprehend the message, teachers can use comic strips for reading instruction. Because they use few words to summarize thoughts and events, teachers can use them to teach inference. Teachers can begin by reading aloud a comic strip to the class, model how to infer meaning from the brief text and the graphic, and then discuss the meaning of the strip (McVicker, 2007). In addition, because they are fun and students can relate to them, comic strips are likely to get the attention of the students.

Besides using comic strips as an alternative to traditional text structure such as narrative texts (storybooks), non-narrative texts (nonfiction), and poetry (McVicker, 2007), Moje (2000) proposed that *graffiti writing* be acknowledged as a literacy approach for developing pedagogies for marginalized students. Graffiti writing, one of many unsanctioned literacy practices of gang-connected students, could be used as a meaning-making, expressive, and communicative tool.

In 3 years of research with five gang-connected students, Moje (2000) discovered that the alternative or unsanctioned literacies these students used included graffiti writing, poetry, narrative, journal writing, letter writing, and novel reading. The gang-connected students used these forms of literacies to construct identities and to position themselves in their gang-connected settings. Moje categorized the literacy practices of the gang-connected students into three types of discourses: *written discourses* (writing of raps, poetry, parodies, letters, and gang symbols), *body discourses* (dress, makeup, hair, hand signs, and body movements), and *oral discourses* (terminologies, accents, and dialects). Although the literacy and language practices of the gang-connected students are often devalued as idle amusements unrelated to school or deemed as violent and deviant, they are important aspects of the everyday practices of some students from poor neighborhoods; as such, teachers need to find ways to support and use such practices to make teaching more relevant to these students. Moje's call for the inclusion of the literacy practices of gang-connected students in school curricula stems from her analysis of gang literacy practices, which she claimed are "remarkably sophisticated," "indicate a high level of metalinguistic awareness," and illustrate "an interest in and motivation to explore language" (p. 680).

Finally, proponents of sociocultural literacy practices recommend *drawing construction*, or the ability to represent text pictorially, as an approach for promoting the reading achievement of students from poverty. Drawing construction requires that readers select important information from the reading, organize selected information into visual images in their mind, and represent the visually organized information as sketches (Bhattacharya, 2007). The effectiveness of drawing construction has been validated by several researchers (e.g., Bhattacharya, 2007; Greene, 1989; Purnell, Ali, Begum, & Carter, 2007; Short, Kauffman, & Kahn, 2000; Van Meter, 2001; Whitin,

2002). Student-generated sketches have the potential of improving students' reading comprehension by acting as mnemonic devices for the retrieval of key information stored in memory from prior reading of text. Teachers therefore could use drawing construction as an approach for promoting the reading of students from impoverished communities.

CONCLUSION

The relationship between poverty and reading achievement has been investigated from a psychosocial perspective and sociocultural perspective. The psychosocial perspective states that family income is predictive of reading achievement and that poverty has an adverse effect on reading achievement. Conversely, the sociocultural perspective asserts that lower reading achievement is not necessarily due to household poverty but rather is often due to a paucity of in-home literacy experiences. Poor students with good in-home literacy experiences tend to exhibit higher reading achievement. Schools can facilitate the reading achievement of poor students by emphasizing home–school partnerships and sociocultural literacy practices. Home–school partnerships can be built by involving parents in literacy education and providing parents with literacy resources and training. Sociocultural literacy practices promote reading development by building on students' experiences and reading materials from the home and community.

The relationship between poverty and reading achievement has been studied through observations, interviews, and surveys. Specifically, family income, literacy resources, parental education, and parenting practices have been studied as home environment factors affecting reading achievement. Future research could examine the relationship between poverty and reading achievement by taking into account the community environment. Poor students' literacy experiences within neighborhood libraries, parks, playgrounds, post offices, supermarkets, and workplaces could be examined to understand the effects of community environment on reading achievement. Students' performances on literacy activities could be evaluated to determine the influence of school–community connections and experiences on reading achievement.

REFERENCES

Avery, N. (2003). The bilingual bag: A middle school reading program that connects the classroom with students' families. *Teaching K-8, 33,* 60–61.

Baker, L. (2003). The role of parents in motivating struggling readers. *Reading & Writing Quarterly: Overcoming Learning Difficulties, 19,* 87–106.

Bernhard, J. K., Cummins, J., Campoy, F. I., Ada, A. F., Winsler, A., & Bleiker, C. (2006). Identity texts and literacy development among preschool English language learners: Enhancing learning opportunities for children at risk for learning disabilities. *Teacher College Record, 108*, 2380–2405.

Bhattacharya, A. (2007). Student drawing and academic language processing. *Academic Exchange Quarterly, 11*, 82–86.

Bradley, R. H., Corwyn, R. F., McAdoo, H. P., & Coll, C. G. (2001). The home environments of children in the United States: Part I. Variations by age, ethnicity, and poverty status. *Child Development, 72*, 1844–1867.

Breitborde, M., & Swiniarski, L. B. (2002). Family education and community power: New structures for new visions in the educational village. *Educational Studies, 28*, 305–318.

Christian, B., & Bloome, D. (2004). Learning to read is who you are. *Reading & Writing Quarterly: Overcoming Learning Difficulties, 20*, 365–384.

Compton-Lilly, C. (2000). Staying on children: Challenging stereotypes about urban parents. *Language Arts, 77*, 420–427.

Compton-Lilly, C. (2006). Identity, childhood culture, and literacy learning: A case study. *Journal of Early Childhood Literacy, 6*, 57–76.

Compton-Lilly, C. (2007). The complexities of reading capital in two Puerto Rican families. *Reading Research Quarterly, 42*, 72–98.

Conley, M. W., & Hinchman, K. A. (2004). No Child Left Behind: What it means for U.S. adolescents and what we can do about it. *Journal of Adolescent and Adult Literacy, 48*, 42–50.

Cooter, K. S. (2006). When mama can't read: Counteracting intergenerational illiteracy. *Reading Teacher, 59*, 698–702.

Cunningham, P. M. (2006). High-poverty schools that beat the odds. *Reading Teacher, 60*, 382–385.

Darling, S. (2008). Family must be part of the solution in closing the achievement gap. *Clearing House, 81*, 245–246.

Dearing, E., Kreider, H., Simpkins, S., & Weiss, H. B. (2006). Family involvement in school and low-income children's literacy: Longitudinal associations between and within families. *Journal of Educational Psychology, 98*, 653–664.

Dever, M. T., & Burts, D. C. (2002). An evaluation of family literacy bags as a vehicle for parent involvement. *Early Child Development and Care, 172*, 359–370.

Dubow, E. F., & Ippolito, M. F. (1994). Effects of poverty and quality of the home environment on changes in the academic and behavioral adjustment of elementary school-age children. *Journal of Clinical Child Psychology, 23*, 401–412.

Duke, N. K., & Purcell-Gates, V. (2003). Genres at home and at school: Bridging the known to the new. *Reading Teacher, 57*, 30–37.

Duke, N. K., Purcell-Gates, V., Hall, L. A., & Tower, C. (2006). Authentic literacy activities for developing comprehension and writing. *Reading Teacher, 60*, 344–355.

Eamon, M. K. (2002). Effects of poverty on mathematics and reading achievement of young adolescents. *Journal of Early Adolescence, 22*, 49–74.

Eamon, M. K. (2005). Socio-demographic, school, neighborhood, and parenting influences on the academic achievement of Latino young adolescents. *Journal of Youth and Adolescence, 34,* 163–174.

Ediger, M. (2008). Psychology of parental involvement in reading. *Reading Improvement, 45,* 46–52.

Edwards, P. A. (1992). Involving parents in building reading instruction for African-American children. *Theory Into Practice, 31,* 350–359.

Evans, G. W. (2004). The environment of childhood poverty. *American Psychologist, 59,* 77–92.

Grande, M. (2004). Increasing parent participation and knowledge using home literacy bags. *Intervention in School and Clinic, 40,* 120–126.

Greene, T. R. (1989). Children's understanding of class inclusion hierarchies: The relationship between external representation and task performance. *Journal of Experimental Child Psychology, 48,* 62–89.

Guo, G. (1998). The timing of the influences of cumulative poverty on children's cognitive ability and achievement. *Social Forces, 77,* 257–288.

Hall, K. (2007). Gator's adventures: A lesson in literacy and community. *Reading Teacher, 60,* 491–493.

Huebner, C. E. (2000). Community-based support for preschool readiness among children in poverty. *Journal of Education for Students Placed at Risk, 5,* 291–314.

Koskinen, P. S., Blum, I. H., Bisson, S. A., Phillips, S. M., Creamer, T. S., & Baker, T. K. (1999). Shared reading, books, and audiotapes: Supporting diverse students in school and at home. *Reading Teacher, 52,* 430–444.

Landis, D., & Moje, E. B. (2003). Introduction: (Re)reading students' difficulties with reading and writing. *Reading & Writing Quarterly: Overcoming Learning Difficulties, 19,* 199–204.

McCarthey, S. J., & Moje, E. B. (2002). Identity matters. *Reading Research Quarterly, 37,* 228–238.

McLoyd, V. C. (1998). Socioeconomic disadvantage and child development. *American Psychologist, 53,* 185–204.

McVicker, C. J. (2007). Comic strips as a text structure for learning to read. *Reading Teacher, 61,* 85–88.

Moje, E. B. (2000). "To be part of the story": The literacy practices of gangsta adolescents. *Teachers College Record, 102,* 651–690.

Moje, E. B. (2002). But where are the youth? On the value of integrating youth culture into literacy theory. *Educational Theory, 52,* 97–120.

Moje, E. B., Dillon, D. R., & O'Brien, D. (2000). Reexamining roles of learners, text, and context in secondary literacy. *Journal of Educational Research, 93,* 165–180.

Moje, E. B., Overby, M., Tysvaer, N., & Morris, K. (2008). The complex world of adolescent literacy: Myths, motivations, and mysteries. *Harvard Educational Review, 78,* 107–154.

Molfese, V. J., Modglin, A., & Molfese, D. L. (2003). The role of environment in the development of reading skills: A longitudinal study of preschool and school-age measures. *Journal of Learning Disabilities, 36,* 59–67.

Molfese, V. J., & Molfese, D. L. (2002). Environmental and social influences on reading skills as indexed by brain and behavioral responses. *Annals of Dyslexia, 52,* 121–137.

Moll, L. C., Amanti, C., Neff, D., & Gonzalez, N. (1992). Funds of knowledge for teaching: Using a qualitative approach to connect homes and classrooms. *Theory Into Practice, 31*, 132–141.

Morrow, L. M., Kuhn, M. R., & Schwanenflugel, P. J. (2006). The family fluency program. *Reading Teacher, 60*, 322–333.

Neuman, S. B. (2006). N is for nonsensical: Low-income preschool children need content-rich instruction, not drill in procedural skills. *Educational Leadership, 64*(2), 28–31.

Nievar, M. A., & Luster, T. (2006). Developmental processes in African American families: An application of McLoyd's theoretical model. *Journal of Marriage and Family, 68*, 320–331.

Ordonez-Jasis, R., & Ortis, R. W. (2006). Reading their worlds: Working with diverse families to enhance children's early literacy development. *Young Children, 61*, 42–48.

Padak, N., & Rasinski, T. (2006). Home-school partnerships in literacy education: From rhetoric to reality. *Reading Teacher, 60*, 292–296.

Padak, N., & Rasinski, T. (2007). Is being wild about Harry enough? Encouraging independent reading at home. *Reading Teacher, 61*, 350–353.

Parcel, T. L., & Dufur, M. J. (2001). Capital at home and at school: Effects on student achievement. *Social Forces, 79*, 881–912.

Powell-Smith, K. A., Shinn, M. R., Stoner, G., & Good, R. H., III. (2000). Parent tutoring in reading using literature and curriculum materials: Impact on student reading achievement. *School Psychology Review, 29*, 5–27.

Purcell-Gates, V. (1996). Stories, coupons, and the *TV Guide*: Relationships between home literacy experiences and emergent literacy knowledge. *Reading Research Quarterly, 31*, 406–428.

Purcell-Gates, V., L'Allier, S., & Smith, D. (1995). Literacy at the Harts' and the Larsons': Diversity among poor inner-city families. *Reading Teacher, 48*, 572–578.

Purnell, P. G., Ali, P., Begum, N., & Carter, M. (2007). Windows, bridges and mirrors: Building culturally responsive early childhood classrooms through the integration of literacy and the arts. *Early Childhood Education Journal, 34*, 419–424.

Rashid, F. L., Morris, R. D., & Sevcik, R. A. (2005). Relationship between home literacy environment and reading achievement in children with reading disabilities. *Journal of Learning Disabilities, 38*, 2–11.

Richardson, M. V., Miller, M. B., Richardson, J. A., & Sacks, M. K. (2008). Literacy bags to encourage family involvement. *Reading Improvement, 45*, 3–9.

Richgels, D. J., & Wold, L. S. (1998). Literacy on the road: Backpacking partnerships between school and home. *Reading Teacher, 52*, 18–19.

Scales, A. M., & Snyder, A. E. (2004). How African American mothers assist their early adolescent daughters with reading tasks. *Reading Psychology, 25*, 297–312.

Share, D., Jorm, A., Maclean, R., Matthews, R., & Waterman, B. (1983). Early reading achievement, oral language ability, and a child's home background. *Australian Psychologist, 18*, 75–87.

Short, K. G., Kauffman, G., & Kahn, L. H. (2000). "I just need to draw": Responding to literature across multiple sign system. *Reading Teacher, 54*, 160–171.

Smith, M. C., & Elish-Piper, L. (2002). Primary-grade educators and adult literacy: Some strategies for assisting low-literate parents. *Reading Teacher*, *56*, 156–165.

Van Meter, P. (2001). Drawing construction as a strategy for learning from text. *Journal of Educational Psychology*, *69*, 129–140.

Waldbart, A., Meyers, B., & Meyers, J. (2006). Invitations to families in an early literacy support program. *Reading Teacher*, *59*, 774–785.

Whitin, P. (2002). Leading into literature circles through the sketch-to-stretch strategy. *Reading Teacher*, *55*, 444–450.

Race, Class, and Schooling: Multicultural Families Doing the Hard Work of Home Literacy in America's Inner City

GUOFANG LI

Michigan State University, East Lansing, Michigan, USA

Drawing on a larger ethnographic study, this article documents (a) how and for what purposes literacy is used in 3 culturally diverse families of low socioeconomic status and (b) what various cultural, socioeconomic, and environmental factors shape the families' literacy practices in their home milieus in an urban context. Data analysis revealed that the families use literacy in both 1st and 2nd languages for a variety of purposes—helping with schoolwork, self-improvement, leisure and everyday living, and advocating for improved school practices. These literacy practices, however, are seriously constrained by various out-of-school factors, such as school–home literacy fracturing, declining neighborhood and school culture, different forms of racism, and family and neighborhood social class statuses. Findings suggest that there is a need to broaden existing efforts to improve minority literacy education within classrooms and schools to address the "limit situations" outside of school that affect students' lives and impede their school achievement. Experts must make a concerted endeavor to improve the urban social and physical environment as well as to implement pedagogical practices that connect students' learning inside school with their lived realities outside school.

In the past few decades, the United States has received different kinds of newcomers—labor, professional, and entrepreneurial immigrants, refugees, and asylum seekers (Portes & Rumbaut, 1996). Although some groups have achieved social mobility and/or ethnic solidarity, many groups of low socioeconomic status (SES), such as refugees and asylum seekers, are rel-egated to poor inner city neighborhoods, which often results in a downward spiral into poverty (McBrien, 2005; Porter & Rumbaut, 1996, 2001). These newly arrived low-SES immigrants and refugees, together with the White working poor remaining in inner cities, have become America's "rainbow underclass." They are highly segregated racially, economically, and residen-tially (Iceland & Scopilliti, 2008); moreover, they are under the impact of a series of social factors such as poverty, racism, negative contexts of reception, and/or language and cultural barriers (Portes & Zhou, 1993).

This racial, residential, and socioeconomic segmentation has a signifi-cant impact on the kinds of schools their children attend and the kind of edu-cation they receive (Kozol, 2004; Li, 2005; Orfield & Lee, 2005). The physical capital of schools—such as the available resources, the social organization of the student population, the teaching force, the learners, and the nature of curriculum and instruction—differ in terms of the SES status of the community (Knapp & Woolverton, 2004; Li, 2005). Schools in higher SES communities tend to possess more physical capital—they attract better quali-fied teachers, receive more resources and funding, and are better equipped with technology (Kozol, 2004; Orfield & Lee, 2005). In contrast, schools serving students from low-income families tend to have fewer resources, experience greater difficulties attracting qualified teachers, and face many more challenges in addressing students' needs (Lee & Burkam, 2002). In addition to the differences in physical capital, schools with different SES sta-tuses also tend to differ in terms of their cultural and symbolic capital, such as leadership, staff morale, expectations for students, and values placed on students' cultures and languages (Suárez-Orozco & Suárez-Orozco, 2001). Suárez-Orozco and Suárez-Orozco discovered that schools serving immigrant and minority children range from high-functioning ones with high expecta-tions and emphases on achievement to catastrophic ones characterized by the ever-present fear of violence, distrust, low expectations, and institutional anomie. The latter, referred to as *fields of endangerment*, are usually located in neighborhoods troubled by drugs, prostitution, and gangs, with families and faculty members focusing on survival.

Racial and economic segregation also correlate with students' achieve-ment gaps. A National Assessment of Educational Progress (NAEP, 2007) report suggests that the achievement gap between different SES groups has been persistent throughout the years. For example, the 2003, 2005, and 2007 results in reading and math indicate that students who are eligible for free or reduced lunch (high poverty) and those who are not (low poverty) turn out to have substantial differences in their achievement. In fact, the aver-age scores of low-SES students have been consistently lower than those of their higher SES peers since the 1990s. In 2007, trends in fourth-grade NAEP average reading scores showed that students who were eligible for free or reduced lunch scored 203 and 215, respectively. In comparison, students who were not eligible scored 232. In addition, 81% of students eligible for free lunch performed at or below the basic level for reading compared to 44% of students who were not eligible. Similar trends have also been observed in fourth-grade math and eighth-grade reading and math and between different racial groups (e.g., between Whites and Blacks; see NAEP, 2007, for the complete report).

Efforts to eliminate poverty and close achievement gaps have focused on studies of effective reading instruction and/or school-wide reforms in high-poverty areas (Fisher & Adler, 2001; Izumi, 2002; Taylor, Pearson, Peterson, & Rodriguez, 2003). Although these efforts have contributed to pockets of success in high-poverty areas, in general they have failed to unpack the effects of other social factors (e.g., race, class, and social context of learning) on the literacy achievement gap (Kainz & Vernon-Feagans, 2007; Li, 2007). As Wamba (2010/this issue) argues, efforts that focus solely on classrooms and schools could well be jeopardized or reversed by what takes place outside the school setting. Researchers have found that it takes more than the quality of teaching to help low-SES children improve literacy achievement. Kainz and Vernon-Feagans, for example, in their longitudinal study of 1,913 economically disadvantaged children from kindergarten to third grade, found that minority racial and economic segregation had a significantly larger effect on the children's long-term reading performance than did the method of instruction. Therefore, to help low-SES minority children achieve school success, it is necessary to move beyond the narrow focus on improving literacy instruction to include examinations of the larger sociocultural, socioeconomic, and socioenvironmental issues that are central to children's everyday lives outside school.

Edmondson and Shannon (1998) suggested that if literacy education is expected to eliminate poverty, it must be tailored theoretically and practically to fit various conceptions of poverty and its causes. In the current global economy, in which having rudimentary reading skills no longer equates with economic success, literacy education must move beyond reading skills instruction to address the development of students' sociological imaginations—ways to rethink their identities in ways that blur the lines between ourselves and others—racially, culturally, and economically (Edmondson & Shannon, 1998). To accomplish this, there is a need to acquire a deep understanding of students' social realities outside school—how and for what purpose literacy is used in their sociocultural milieus, and how different factors such as family, neighborhood, race, and SES are related to their academic achievement in school.

Drawing on a larger ethnographic study, this article examines the socio-cultural factors and literacy practices that influence the educational experiences of three low-SES families. These families are from three racial and ethnic groups (Sudanese, Vietnamese, and White Euro-American), and they live in western New York. This ethnographic study explores both (a) the rich complexity of reading and writing practices within each family as family members make sense of their daily relations in terms of race, ethnicity, and class; and (b) the productions of such relations across cultural groups and within the contexts of low-SES neighborhoods and schools and larger sociocultural and socioeconomic formations. The study was guided by two research questions: (a) What is literacy like in the three families' home milieus? and (b) What different cultural, socioeconomic, and environmental factors shape the families' home literacy practices and school achievement, and how do they do so?

THEORETICAL FRAMEWORK

In this article, *literacy* means "an identity kit"—a discourse characterized by socially accepted ways of using language, of thinking, and of acting (Gee, 1991, p. 3). According to Foucault (1978), a discourse is not just a language system; it also constitutes power relations and invokes particular notions of truth and thus defines what is acceptable and unacceptable in a given context. As such, power is executed less through physical instruments but through discursive formations among various sociocultural elements such as race, ethnicity, and class (Foucault, 1972).

Literacy discourses are intrinsically diverse, historically and culturally viable, social practices (Collins & Blot, 2003). Research on language socialization has indicated that language and literacy learning is part of a process of socialization through which the learner acquires particular values and relationships in these diverse discourses in which learning takes place (Schieffelin & Ochs, 1986). Ochs (1986) posited that children acquire a worldview as they acquire a language. Because the process of acquiring language is deeply affected by the process of becoming a competent member of a community, language and literacy learning is intricately linked to the construction of social roles, cultural affiliations, beliefs, values, and social practices (Schieffelin & Ochs, 1986). For language-minority learners who traverse two cultural worlds, the process of acquiring language(s) and literacies may involve the intersection of multiple/different cultural values and beliefs and multiple social practices. For such learners, as Lam (2004) observed, it is important to note that language and literacy practices do not exist in isolation from one another just as cultures and communities do not exist as discrete entities, but rather interact with one another in various degrees of complementarity or conflict.

In this study, the families' literacy practices and learning experiences are viewed as a social construction and as part of the process of becoming culturally competent members of their communities. The analysis of the families' literacy practices is linked to more general ethnographic accounts of cultural beliefs and practices as the families form certain social relations (e.g., in terms of race and class) with schools and the communities in which they reside. This article explores how these culturally different families contest institutional constraints, resist discrimination, countermand the adversarial context of the inner city, and traverse the narrow path toward success.

METHOD

The Families and Their Children

The three families included in this study are the Torkeri family (Sudanese), the Ton family (Vietnamese), and the Sassano family (White American).

The Torkeri family originally came to the United States in 1999 from a southern city of Sudan called Juba. The mother, Anne, who almost completed her degree in teacher education in Sudan, stayed home to take care of the children while the father, Tifa, who had been trained as a lawyer in Egypt, now worked as a welder for 40 hr a week to support the family. He earned about $11.79 per hour. He slept about 4 hr a day and rose very early every morning to fix used cars to make extra money. In addition to supporting their family in the United States, Anne and Tifa also sent about $100 a month to Anne's mother and sister, who were taking refuge in Egypt. There were six children in the family: Owen (15 years of age), Nina (13), Fred (11), Irene (6), Jude (3), and Igma (8 months). Owen attended a nearby high school (in 2006, it was characterized by a population of 88% African American and 47% eligible for free and reduced lunch; only 30.9% of graduates earned a Regents diploma from the New York Department of Education), and Nina and Fred attended Rainbow Elementary. Whereas Nina and Irene were doing well in school, Owen and Fred were struggling in school. Owen and Fred had been in an English as a second language (ESL) pullout program, with Fred also receiving special education services. The eight family members lived in an upper level two-bedroom apartment situated in an unkempt two-story house.

The Ton family came to the United States in 1993 from Vietnam. Lo and Cam both finished Grade 11 in a Vietnamese high school. Lo (the father) could speak conversational English with a heavy accent, and Cam (the mother) spoke only minimal English, such as general greetings. Both were hired to do embroidery work in a hat factory in the city. Lo and Cam had three children: their first son Mien, who was 14; daughter Nyen who was 12; and another son, Dan, who was 8. Whereas Mien and Nyen were doing well in school, Dan struggled with English and other academic subjects. All children attended Rainbow Elementary. The family had lived in an apartment for 4 years and bought their two-story house in the same neighborhood in 1998.

The Sassano family was local to the city and was one of the few White families remaining in the neighborhood. At the time of the study, Loraine Sassano worked as a part-time clerk in the meat department at a local grocery store while studying at the community college to become a nurse. Her husband Stanley worked as a local jeweler. For a period of time, they had also applied for social welfare but had been denied. They had two sons: Scott was 13 and in seventh grade, and Rod was 10 and in fourth grade. Scott and Rod both attended Rainbow Elementary, where they were among the few American-born White students in the school. Scott had been on the merit roll in the school and had been admitted to Madison Tech, a good high school, in 2005, but he was having a hard time coping academically in the high school. Rod had been on the honor roll in Rainbow Elementary school with a 90% grade point average, but according to Loraine, he started to "regress" like his brother between 2004 and 2006.

Data Collection

Semistructured interviews and participant observations were used to provide rich descriptive data about the contexts, activities, and beliefs of the families (Creswell, 2005). Families were selected from Rainbow Elementary, a local international elementary school designated for refugees. Participants in the current study were part of a larger study on the school and home literacy connections of fourth-grade students (Li, 2008). During May 2004 and July 2006, my research assistant and I visited the Torkeri, Ton, and Sassano families and carried out observations and interviews. The Torkeris and the Tons were visited more than six times, and the Sassano family was visited four times. We were also invited to attend church events and cultural activities with these families. The number of telephone conversations with the three families varied depending on our rapport.

All three families were formally interviewed twice at their houses during the research process, once at the beginning and once at the end of the research process. At least one parent and the older children in each family were interviewed. The two interviews were conducted as a means of understanding the families' beliefs and values about their children's education and of gaining more specific information about their literacy practices (in terms of their access to literacy materials and their uses) as well as their thoughts on race, class, and cultural differences. At times, because of language barriers, the children were occasionally asked to translate some of the questions and answers. In addition to these interviews, observations and casual conversations with the participants were also conducted and recorded in field notes. Two participant observations for each family took place at the same time as the formal interviews. Other observations occurred during the research process, and the frequency of observation varied depending on the availability of the families. The purposes of these observations were to understand the children's home literacy environments (e.g., the amount and type of print materials), their language use, their interaction with siblings and adults, their reading and writing activities, their computer use, and their TV watching habits in the home setting. My role (and that of my research assistant) during the observations varied depending on the context of the activities. For example, I was more of an observer when the children played among themselves. At other times I was more of a participant (e.g., when the family all sat in their living room watching TV in their native language). In addition to the three families, three teachers, a parent liaison, a school site facilitator, and a community activist were interviewed to better understand the school, community, and neighborhood contexts for the project. Each of the interviews lasted approximately 2 hr and was audiotaped and subsequently transcribed.

Data Analysis

Data analysis was ongoing throughout the data collection period. Two complementary methods were used to analyze data. Following Glaser and Strauss's (1967) grounded theory approach, the transcripts and field notes were first coded using open coding methods. Open coding allowed for the identification of major concepts and the emergence of categories related to literacy practices. Examples of these categories include literacy practice, interaction with school, interaction with the system, immigration, cultural differences, and work. After this initial coding, the data chunks were further coded into smaller categories. For example, in the literacy practice category, several other codes were developed, such as reading, writing, mathematics, and language use. In the cultural differences category, further themes were identified, such as culture, parenting, community support, and schooling difference. Based on the identified patterns, a table of contents that contained bigger themes was created to visualize the data in a categorical organization for each family. Themes and data chunks relating to the research questions were also identified and categorized for each family. This step allowed for a better demonstration of the "true value of the original multiple realities" (Lincoln & Guba, 1985, p. 296) through the use of direct quotes from the formal and informal interviews to give voice to the participants. Once the coding was completed for each family, a cross-case analysis was conducted to determine both the uniqueness and the commonality of three families' experiences (Merriam, 1998). This second method of analysis consisted of a cross-case search for patterns and themes that were related to the two research questions. This analysis allows for the development of more sophisticated descriptions of the families' home literacy practices and more powerful explanations of the various factors that affected the children's learning at home and in school (Creswell, 2005).

FINDINGS

This section first provides a detailed account of the three families' literacy practices. It describes how and for what purposes literacy is used in the families to address the first research question (What is literacy like in the three families' home milieus?). This provides a context for understanding the various out-of-school factors that influence the students' achievement. Following this, an analysis is presented of the different out-of-school factors that shape the families' home literacy practices and schooling in the inner city context to address the second research question (What different cultural, socioeconomic, and environmental factors shape the families' home literacy practices and school achievement, and how do they do so?).

Home Literacy Practices in the Families

As indicated in the family profiles, although the immigrant parents had different levels of education prior to coming to America, they all had very low levels of English proficiency. In addition, they, along with the native-born White parents, had low-wage jobs in factories, shops, and grocery stores. Despite their low incomes, all households reported using literacy for a variety of purposes—school homework, self-improvement, entertainment and leisure, and fighting against school practices (Farr, 1994; Purcell-Gates, 1996; Reese, 2009).

THE ROLE OF SCHOOL IN HOME LITERACY PRACTICES

The data analysis suggested that reading and writing for school-related purposes was one of the major domains for which literacy was used in the homes of the three culturally different families. Similar to in prior studies (e.g., Reese, 2009), in this study school-promoted activities included helping with homework; reading with children; reading notes and fliers from the school or teacher; and creating study materials, such as math homework, to assist the child with learning.

In the Torkeri family, because Tifa worked most of the time, Anne, who had been trained as a teacher in Sudan, was responsible for checking the children's homework. Everyday when the children returned from school, Anne asked them about their day at school and checked their backpacks to see what homework was required for that evening. The children usually watched TV or played on their old computer while she prepared supper. After supper, Anne asked everyone to clean up the dining table and their coffee table to make space for their homework. When they were studying, no eating or drinking was allowed, because it might ruin their books and notebooks. Anne believed that it was important to "do one thing at a time."

Irene, who went to a Head Start program, received a lot of attention from Anne, as her homework required Anne's involvement. Anne usually read with her first. Their routine was that Irene read the book and, if she experienced trouble reading an unknown word, Anne helped her figure it out by referring to a dictionary. After reading, Anne asked Irene to copy the words. If she did not write neatly, Anne made her redo it. Anne also helped Irene practice her spelling. She often tested Irene by asking, "Can you spell this word?" Sometimes Anne sounded out the words to help Irene spell or pronounce a word. She modeled the pronunciation and asked Irene to repeat after her. At times, she also used pictures to help Irene understand difficult words. In addition to reading and writing, Anne played card games with Irene to teach her numbers, colors, animals, and fruits. She also played Scrabble, a word game, with her to increase her vocabulary. Sometimes Anne and Irene invented new games to play. For example, one day Irene pretended that her mother was not there and she had to take care of all her young siblings. Anne wrote down Irene's story about her taking care of her brothers and sisters, and they read it together.

Anne tried to do the same thing with Fred, who was required to read 20 min a day for his school assignment, but it was very difficult to get him to read because of his learning disabilities. Most of the time, Anne just let him copy the words and then she corrected it: "I'll let him know which one is right, which one is wrong. After that, the wrong one, he has to write it like three times so that he may remember the mistaken word." In addition to writing, Anne also helped Fred with math:

> But the only thing I'm very poor is with the math. I can't help them with math. Only this one [Fred]. I help him with the multiplication. I wrote the multiplication up to 12. And then, every day I have to test him for… multiplication of 2, and then the following day, 3, and then, so all until he finish with it.

For Owen and Nina, who were older, Anne just "let them do it by themselves first" and then checked later "if they [were] doing it right or wrong." As for Nina, Anne noted that she often forgot to hand in her homework, even though she had completed it. Sometimes Nina (and Fred) forgot to bring their homework to school, and Anne had to "run to the school to take it to them." Although most of the time Anne enlisted Owen's help with difficult words or math problems, she tried her best to be actively involved with his homework as well. She tried to review his major assignments before he handed them in. When reviewing some of his essays, she taught him that the way he wrote should be different from the way he spoke; she also pointed out some spelling errors, asking him to check the dictionary.

In the Ton family, because the older children, Mien and Nyen, were doing well in school, Lo and Cam focused their effort on helping Dan whenever they had time. According to Lo, Dan could "speak but he [could not] write and read." Moreover, Dan was also slow in math. Though Lo and Cam were very worried and felt they could not help Dan academically, they also did not know how to go to the school to ask mainstream teachers for help. Lo explained, "Very hard sometimes. I don't speak [English] very well,

I don't know how to talk to the teacher. He [the teacher] got another child, you know." Everyday when Dan came home, Lo would check his bookbag to see if he had any homework. Usually, the teacher would send home a book for Dan to read. Lo was always surprised by this homework, as he noted that Dan "didn't know nothing about book. He know some words like easy word, like two letters, that's he know, like *we, yes* he know, he cannot know long word." In order to teach Dan how to read, Lo and Cam first read the letters to Dan. Lo described it like this:

> I still read him the letter, I read first and he follow me. We did it one time he'll tell me that if he don't know, he cannot read alone...I let him read until he can read the book.

They also bought some reading toys, such as the Leopard Learning System, so that Dan could see the words and listen to the sounds and read after it. In order to help Dan commit words to memory, they decided to have him copy each word five times. Each night they selected 10 words from his homework book and asked him to copy. Lo believed that copying was a very effective method: "[If] he is not writing, he [does] not remember... While I say, write a word he know, he cannot say that, he cannot write, but he see it, he can write." Sometimes Lo and Cam would ask the older children to help. In terms of math, Lo and Cam noticed that even though Dan was not good at math, he had very little math homework. Therefore, they created additional math homework as extra practice. Lo admitted that he was not sure how to help his son improve in math, but he could not express this to Dan's teacher: "I don't know how to teach math. I try help him. How I want to say to teacher?"

In the Sassano family, the parents established a very strict homework-first policy. For example, the two children, Rod and Scott, understood that "they have to do homework immediately, that's automatic." Loraine explained, "After school...when they walk in the door, homework has to be done, so that they can do anything [after that]." In addition to making sure the children do their homework, Loraine also checked all their homework. Her principle was that she did not change anything they wrote, even if it was wrong. However, she did point out that there were errors and asked them to locate and correct them. She believed that they needed to learn from their own mistakes. She also paid attention to their handwriting, and if it was illegible, she would ask them to rewrite their work.

As these families' homework practices illustrate, the families tried their best to respond to school demands either by themselves or by enlisting their more capable children to help. Even if the parents were busy or did not know English, they all reported being involved in their children's homework to varying degrees—either supervising or checking the homework—and they took their children's homework seriously.

LITERACY FOR SELF-IMPROVEMENT, ENJOYMENT, AND EVERYDAY LIVING

Because all of the parents worked in low-wage jobs that required minimal reading and writing skills, they rarely reported bringing home work-related literacy materials or tasks. However, in the families, the parents' drive to improve their own education generated different literacy activities at home. For example, Loraine Sassano, a high school graduate, had decided to further her education to become a nurse. As a student attending classes at the community college, Loraine usually studied and did her homework together with the boys. She read her textbooks and did homework, writing reports and research papers in the evenings, and thus was "on the computer all the time."

In addition to the school-related literacy activities, the families also reported using literacy for leisure and entertainment. Whereas the White parents read and wrote in English only, the immigrant parents read (and wrote) in both English and their first languages.

In the Sassano family, Loraine was an avid reader who read a lot of medical mysteries. She expressed her love of reading as follows: "I could spend all day in a book." She hoped that her love of reading would "rub off" on her children. There were books and reading materials everywhere in their house. Loraine always bought the kids new books or took them to the public library to borrow books. She emphasized, "Whenever they ask for a book, I never say no." No matter how tight their budget was, she and her husband would take them to the bookstore and buy the books they wanted or needed. Rod, a fourth grader, was also an avid reader. Like his mother, he enjoyed reading mystery books and loved chapter books such as *Fudge*, a popular book by Judy Blume.

Though the other families did not report a similar zest for leisure reading or a similar attitude toward buying books, data from the interviews and home visits indicated that the families read for different leisure and entertainment purposes at home. The Ton parents usually read two Vietnamese newspapers published in Toronto, *Saigon Canada* and *Thoi Bao* (*Vietnamese Weekly*), which they bought from a nearby Vietnamese grocery store. In addition to these weekly readings, they also read news in Vietnamese on the Internet as a means of remaining updated with what was happening in Vietnam and the world. Sometimes they also browsed some English materials of interest. For example, the Tons sometimes bought English newspapers.

Because the Torkeri family did not have access to the Internet at home or print materials in their first languages, they relied on Sudanese/African television to keep in touch with Sudanese and African news. In the Torkeri family, leisure reading also included materials related to their American dreams. For example, Tifa, who wanted to become an auto mechanic, liked to read books and articles from magazines such as *Quality Black Enterprise* that often reported stories of successful Black people.

In addition to this pleasure reading, all families read a variety of print materials for everyday living. For the families, who lived on tight budgets, reading flyers and looking for coupons for groceries or everyday necessities was a very common practice. The families also read a variety of documents, such as immigration papers, birth certificates, mortgage or insurance papers, bank statements, and application forms for housing and welfare support. They also wrote letters and/or e-mails to relatives in English and/or in their first languages.

As described previously, the parents took the children's schooling and home-work seriously. However, they were not uniformly accepting of school practices. In fact, some of the reading and writing homework often became sources of critique of the urban school practices and resistance to the school system. For example, the Torkeris, the Sudanese parents, believed that the American schools were not rigorous in their general knowledge instruction and math curriculum.

These critiques sometimes prompted the families to resist school sanctions and practices that they deemed unfavorable to their children's literacy learning. The Torkeris, for example, believed that the ESL pullout programs were detrimental to their children's literacy learning, as the children often missed the main classroom instruction as a consequence of being pulled out. They had gone to Parent–Teacher Association meetings and raised these issues along with other refugee parents. They requested that the school restructure the ESL program by offering classes after school. However, their plea was not heard, even though they asked their community leader to write a letter to the school on their behalf. After a series of failed efforts, the family decided to keep silent with the school while seeking other ways to take their children out of the ESL programs. Anne Torkeri presented the matter to City Hall and requested that Owen be taken off the ESL list and allowed to take the English Language Arts test. In addition, she applied to other schools on behalf of her younger children, who had been born in the United States, believing that they should be treated as Americans and therefore be exempted from ESL programs. Through what she called a "lottery drawing" at City Hall, where she filled out the application forms and awaited random school assignment, she successfully got her daughter Irene (and later Jude) admitted to a school in a much better neighborhood where they would not be enrolled in ESL classes.

Similarly, when Scott Sassano's bio-lab teacher repeatedly misplaced Scott's homework and his grade point average fell to a C, Loraine made a point to save his homework on her computer so that she could keep track of what he had completed. When the lab teacher informed her again that Scott did not have his lab reports, Loraine told him that she had all the reports on her computer, and she asked Scott to reprint and hand them in the next day. She also called the principal and reported the problem. The principal then arranged the lab reports to be handed in to the Vice Principal, and Loraine demanded a receipt from the Vice Principal. Since then, no lab reports had been reported missing. However, Loraine's fight did not stop there. After she learned that many other students had similar problems, she asked Scott to tell all of his classmates that they should turn everything in to their guidance counselor or the Vice Principal and have them sign off and provide a receipt. She hoped that this would encourage the school to recognize that a problem existed and that they must find a solution.

The families' critique of and resistance to school practices signify their resistance to the cultural narratives that frame them as "deficient" or "uncaring" (Rogers, 2003). These "alternative discourses," however, do not always result in their "getting somewhere" in terms of school success (Compton-Lilly, 2002, p. 123). As the next section demonstrates, the families' literacy practices were also subject to the influence of a myriad of sociocultural and socioeconomic factors.

Factors That Influence the Families' Home Literacy Practices and School Achievement

As described previously, the three culturally diverse families used literacy in their first and second languages for a wide array of purposes in their homes. Central to these practices were the parents' responses to school demands—both for and against school practices. These practices, however, were subject to the influence of different cultural, socioeconomic, and environmental elements, such as school–home literacy mismatch, a declining neighborhood, race relations and racism, and family social class status.

HOME AND SCHOOL LITERACY FRACTURING

The data analysis suggested that all the three families experienced various degrees of educational and cultural displacement that in turn resulted in different levels of "fracturing" in their literacy practices characterized by different demands on language use and cultural practices in school and at home (Vélez-Ibáñez & Greenberg, 2005).

In the two immigrant families, home literacy was characterized by the extensive use of the families' first languages (i.e., Vietnamese, Bari, and Dinka) and the fact that the parents, with varying levels of English proficiency, did not speak English at home. Their use of first languages, however, was frequently fractured by increasing demands from school and the larger society that their children embrace English literacy at the cost of their own heritage languages. All of the parents wanted their children to be literate in their first languages. However, only the older children had the ability to speak in their native tongue; the younger children increasingly refused to learn to speak it or to associate themselves with their first-language identities. The growing language fracturing or gaps between parents (and grandparents) and the younger children resulted in the parents becoming unable to participate (or participate effectively) in the children's schoolwork. In some cases, when the children failed to learn English in school, the parents who did not speak English themselves succumbed to this process of fracturing by not speaking/teaching their first language to their children out of the concern that it would interfere with the children's acquisition of English.

In some cases, this literacy fracturing also occurred in school settings when the teachers failed to understand the students' language and cultural backgrounds and their specific needs in language and literacy learning. For example, the Torkeris, although they came from Sudan and did not speak any Arabic, were sent to an Arabic-speaking teacher for help. This profound lack of knowledge about the students' language and cultural backgrounds was another catalyst for literacy fracturing that not only contributed to the children's underachievement but also added to the psychosocial stressors they experienced in school.

Another example of literacy fracturing was the common message that the parents often received from school—"Read with your child." In the Vietnamese family, for example, the Ton parents' inability to speak English prevented them from participating in their children's literacy activities or being able to be involved in their homework. They were unable to "read" to their children as the teachers had demanded, nor could they "read" in the way the teachers implied—in the form of Eurocentric, parent–child shared reading. For them, "read with your child" meant the child reads and the adult supervises them, as the parents often spoke little English and with a heavy accent that they did not want their children to acquire. In the Sudanese family, though Anne Torkeri had some time to spend with her children and was able to read with her daughter Irene, their reading was also an adult-supervised reading practice.

In the Sassano family, literacy fracturing was manifested differently. The mismatch was more about reading "for fun" or "for duty." Although the school emphasized the efferent stance of reading—that is, reading for information and for the accomplishment of an assigned task—the Sassano children preferred a more aesthetic stance—reading for pleasure and/or for the lived experience through reading (Rosenblatt, 2004). Though Rod Sassano was sometimes able to make that connection, as he understood the importance of doing homework, his brother Scott was often unable to translate between the two stances. As a result, Scott was often reticent to "read for reading's sake."

A DECLINING NEIGHBORHOOD

In addition to the school and home literacy mismatch, the declining neighborhood was another important factor in shaping the families' home literacy practices. The neighborhood in which the families resided had once been a nice neighborhood with mostly middle- and working-class Italian residents. Over the years, the widespread drug use and violence had made it a notorious "war zone" for gangs (Thomas, 2006). As the Whites started to flee the city, the neighborhood became a multiethnic area filled with low-SES African Americans, immigrants, and refugees. It had also become a very transient place whose population was in a constant state of flux. This transient nature had, to some degree, made the neighborhood a dangerous place to live. As Marilyn, a site facilitator for some urban school initiatives, explained,

> And it has gone downhill. My understanding is [it went] very quickly. I think about 99% of the kids that attend my school are considered to be living in poverty. And that's defined by their eligibility for free or reduced lunches...High crime, a lot of gang activity, a lot of drugs, a lot of gun-running, that sort of thing. It comes out of [this neighborhood]. The kids grow up in this sort of environment...The corner of our school...is supposed to be one of the worst places for drug trafficking.

The increasingly dangerous environment seriously influenced the children's learning in school and home. Some of the Torkeri children had witnessed a murder scene on their way from school. The Sassanos lived by a high school, so they witnessed fights and violence almost everyday from their doorstep. In 2004 and 2005, Scott and Rod witnessed a few more shooting incidents and drug raids from their porch and saw bullets flying by. One time they recalled watching police pull three Black men out of their car, finding what looked to be huge bricks of a white drug in the car. As Loraine described, it was like "watching a movie, except it's happening right outside their house in my neighborhood. My kids are SITTING RIGHT THERE!"

These incidents suggest that the neighborhood indeed had become a "field of endangerment" for the children (Suárez-Orozco & Suárez-Orozco, 2001). All of the parents reported making an effort to know their children's whereabouts. The Vietnamese Ton parents forbade their daughters to go out on their own while making an effort to drive their sons to and from their friends' houses. The Sudanese Torkeri parents forbade their children to join many of the after-school activities at school because they were concerned that they might join in some gang activities. As a result, most of the children were confined to their homes most of the time, playing on their own or watching TV.

The transient nature of the neighborhood also meant that student populations in the schools changed constantly. In Rainbow Elementary, for example, around 25% of the student population had been transferred to the school, and the average classroom could suffer a 35% change in its makeup over the course of a school year. Because of budget cuts within the school, there were fewer teachers, but the number of students continued to increase. The number of students per class had increased from 20 to 30 in the past couple of years, and sometimes many of these students had no prior schooling experiences. For many teachers, diversity was a good thing, but it was also a real challenge, as they often ended up "with a new problem every minute, every hour." Therefore, as one teacher commented, teaching in the school was "just being able to survive from day to day with those big problems you have."

The declining community culture also influenced the school culture. According to the Sassano children, the culture in the school "had gotten worse," and picking on people and fighting became the school norm. Rod, for example, could not believe that in his class when one student's father died, other students made fun of it. He believed that all of this was happening because of a general lack of caring and respect in the community. He further explained,

> People have just been worse; people just don't care any more … They just are bad … Fight, scream … People just punch people. They don't care. They don't really care. Teachers are just as bad … Shout the kids down.

Scott was also very pessimistic about the city schools, including his own high school, which was one of the better schools. He commented, "All the city schools are going down … ' cause everyone disrespects everything."

In 2006, Rainbow Elementary School cut some of its bilingual teachers and aides, such as the Vietnamese teacher. The cut created a huge problem for the Vietnamese Ton family, who relied on the bilingual teacher for information regarding their children in school and for communicating with the school administrators and content area teachers. The Ton family relied on the Vietnamese teacher to pass on their complaint that there was not enough math homework because their young son, Dan, was struggling with math. They also relied on the Vietnamese teacher to tutor Dan in English reading and writing and to instruct them on how to assist Dan with his academics at home. Lo Ton expressed his disappointment at the school's decision to cut the Vietnamese teacher: "I want Vietnamese teacher there because of a lot of Vietnamese kids like Dan … We … parents don't know how to speak English … After Mrs. Hon (the Vietnamese teacher), who [will] help?"

Another big influence on the children's literacy practices was the closing of the public library in the neighborhood in 2005 due to city budget cuts. All of the families reported having used the library to borrow books and other materials. All of the families reported that after the closing of the library, they had nowhere else to go to borrow books. Except for the Sassanos, who continued to buy books for their children, the families reported having to rely on the school for reading materials. The closing of the library, therefore, severely limited their access to books and reduced their children's exposure to reading materials.

RACE RELATIONS AND RACISM

In addition to the neighborhood, the complex race relations in the city influenced the children's learning in and out of school. The declining economy and the rising violence and drugs within the city worsened relations between the Blacks and the Whites. In the neighborhood in which the families resided, there was a big divide between poor Whites and other racial minorities such as Blacks and Hispanics. Whereas the Whites blamed the Blacks for the existing urban problems, the Blacks saw themselves as victims of White racism. The racial and economic tensions had significantly influenced the making of the school systems in the city. Within the city, racial concentrations became the index for school achievement. The whiter the school, the better the academic achievement. All of the children in the three families, except for the Irene and Jude Torkeri, attended schools with more than 70% Black students and more than a 90% poverty rate.

Race relations influenced how the children were taught to think, act, and use socially appropriate language at home and in school (Gee, 1989). Although the Sudanese family shared a similar skin color to that of native-born African Americans, they clearly differentiated themselves from them. Tifa Torkeri commented, "The way how we look at things, me and Anne and the kids will be different, the value here and the values in Sudan, the different place." In order to resist the racial stereotypes that others had about Blacks (e.g., as troublemakers who were responsible for the prevalent drug use and violence in the city and society), the Sudanese parents made an effort to educate their children to value education and the chances they had in America, that is, to learn to read and write English, go to college, and seek better job opportunities—what White America defined as its prerogatives (Fordham, 1996). As Anne Torkeri noted, "There are things like that happening. But still there is chance. Why do you give up that for education?" They also taught their children to "do good" and act respectfully to others (e.g., by smiling at people and talking to people nicely), especially the Whites in society, to change their perceptions of them as Blacks. Tifa explained,

> [If] you do something good, then people love you despite the color of your skin...It depend on the way how you are dealing with people ...I'm always telling them that...because...we as Black people in the U.S., we notice so many bad habit coming from us, so mostly if you are dealing with some people who are not Black like you, they will be hesitant. Sometimes the person will come to their mind with bad things, but you have to prove to them that not all Black people are like that by doing good things.

The children also viewed themselves as different from native-born Blacks because they talked differently, ate different foods, and liked different sports. They also understood that they were treated differently from Whites.

At the other end of the spectrum, race relations played out differently for the White families, who were racial minorities in the neighborhood and poor. Their identity was that of "being not-black, not-Asian, not-Latino...not-'ethnic' as well as not-rich-white" (Perry, 2002, p. 182). Because of this unique identity, they experienced bullying and discrimination in the school and the community. For example, in school Black children often picked on the Sassano children. Rod believed that this happened because the Black students hated him for being White and for disagreeing with their behaviors in school. According to Rod, the Black students called him "a nigger" or sometimes "Chinese" and hit him. He said,

> They don't care. They call everyone whatever...they call White people whatever that bad word...A lot of students in my class are racists...They don't really pick on Black people. They pick on White people and Puerto Ricans.

As Loraine Sassano noted, Rod and Scott "got to taste what [it] is like to be on the other side." Their negative experiences in the school had seriously discouraged Rod's and Scott's motivation to learn and their desire to go to school. As their treatment in school worsened, their performance started to decline. Rod, who had been on the honor roll, regressed to the merit role, and Scott fell to a C average. When the children started to have so many problems in school, Loraine went to speak with the principals. Her frequent visits to the schools made her feel fed up and frustrated with what was occurring in the schools and the city. Realizing that they had to put a stop to all these problems, in 2006 the Sassanos decided to join the "White flight" and moved to a White suburb. They believed the schools there would not allow students like Scott and Rod to have the same experiences and fall through the cracks.

On the margin of the Black and White divide, the Vietnamese Tons, as Asians, were often excluded from the dominant racial discourse. However, the family was also socialized into accepting the prevalent racial stereotypes that "the Blacks are troublemakers and Whites are good people, and the Asians are the quiet and hardworking." To them, as the Ton parents noted, "Talk make[s] trouble...Talk too much is [to] have trouble. No talk, no trouble." They encouraged their children to socialize within Vietnamese circles. Their attitudes were also reflected in the children's relationships with students from other ethnic groups. Mien hung out with only Vietnamese friends, and both Nyen and Dan did not like some of the African students in the school. Nyen said that "some of them are mean. They annoy me a lot at school. Sometimes they get me in trouble...For something I didn't do. They said they'd hit me." Dan added that "Africans kind of make trouble" and sometimes they say "F words." Even though the Vietnamese considered Whites "nice people," they also kept a social distance. Lo Ton, for example, was aware that racism existed in society: "Sometime(s), they [White Americans] don't want Vietnamese . . . the boss . . . they don't like Vietnamese people." Lo believed that it had to do with Vietnamese people's language skills:

> I think that American people, they born here. They speak very well . . . So we, like me, I don't know how to speak very well . . . Sometimes they [Americans] make trouble, I can't complain them. I don't know how to speak. That's why, that's not fair.

These incidents suggest that these racially different families and students were traveling on parallel racial tracks though living and studying in the same schools and neighborhood. Similar to the students in Olsen's (1997) study, these students were "separated—immigrants from U.S. born, racial group from racial group—both socially and academically, where students who can't speak English are shut out of opportunities to learn and make contact with their American schoolmates" (p. 10). For these students, as Olsen pointed out, to acquire good English literacy skills alone was not enough to make it in America; they also needed to accomplish another major task—to figure out the peculiar meanings of racial categories in America and learn how to negotiate their own positioning on this racial map.

SOCIAL CLASS

The issue of race and race relations was further compounded by the families' social class backgrounds. As described earlier, the parents all worked in low-wage jobs, such as factory worker and technician. However, some of the immigrant families, such as the Torkeris, came from middle-class backgrounds in their countries of origin and experienced a status drop in America. In a sense, they became "the middle-class poor people" in America (Sampson, 2003). The socioeconomic features they developed in their countries of origin, however, continued to shape their lives in America (Fuligni & Yoshikawa, 2003). In contrast to the popular belief that low-SES families do not care for their children's education, all of the families had high educational expectations for their children. They all expected their children to go to college to receive a higher education.

The families' contradictory class statuses (i.e., as middle class and poor) shaped what the families could do to improve their children's learning at home. The families, like those middle-class families described in Lareau's (2003) study, actively sought opportunities to cultivate their children's learning outside school. For example, the Torkeri family relied on the local church and other charity organizations and sent Nina, Owen, and Fred to a couple of summer camps and on camping trips for free. They also actively participated in church activities in which the children could play music, sports, and become active members of the community. The Ton family tried to take their children on road trips (e.g., to Boston and Canada to see their relatives). The Sassanos enrolled their children in Boy Scouts activities so that they could go camping, hiking, and fishing and learn about team work. They also relied on their relatives (e.g., Loraine's brother-in-law) for financial help to go on family vacations. In Bourdieu's (1977) terms, these efforts no doubt exposed the children to a variety of literacy activities and helped them accumulate the "cultural capital" that is believed to be conducive to school learning.

Their efforts at the concerted cultivation of middle-class cultural capital, however, were heavily constrained by their social class realities in America. Being poor severely limited what the families could do to accumulate cultural capital. In the immigrant families, though all of the parents wanted to spend more time with their children and to help with homework, their busy work schedule and economic pressure did not allow them to take time off work. In these families, all of the parents worked long hours and rarely could afford not to work. As a result, they had much less time to spend with their children than did their middle-class counterparts in the suburbs.

In all of the families, economic pressure limited the families' abilities to move out of the neighborhood and the schools even if they desired to do so. All of these families were unsatisfied with the neighborhood and its schools. However, they had to stay there, as they could not afford to live anywhere else (except for the Sassanos, who moved out with the financial help of their relatives in 2006). In order to move out of the area, the Torkeris, for example, decided to do 500 hr of community service for Habitat for Humanity in exchange for securing a house with a low mortgage, and they were still far from reaching their targeted hours. Poverty, therefore, not only shaped the families' literacy lives but also refused them access to better schools and neighborhoods, which in turn put them at a disadvantage in terms of achieving literacy (Hicks, 2002; Shannon, 1998).

DISCUSSIONS AND CONCLUSIONS

This article has described the multifaceted home literacy practices in three culturally diverse families and the various factors that shaped those literacy practices. As their stories demonstrate, despite the families' lower SES, their homes were print rich, with a wide range of literacy materials available, and the families used literacy resources for a variety of purposes (e.g., pleasure, school, everyday living). They also tried to engage their children in a variety of cultural activities to accumulate middle-class cultural capital.

However, the adversities of cultural and contextual barriers, such as school–home literacy fracturing, racism, and family and neighborhood SES, became "limit situations" that constrained the families' home literacy practices and impeded the children's school achievement (Freire, 1970, p. 89). These barriers suggest that that these members of America's "underclass" do not ascribe to the "culture of poverty" or choose inadequate schools or neighborhoods; rather, it is these limit situations and constraints that put them at a social and class disadvantage.

To help low-SES families and children such as those in this study overcome these barriers, experts must address the sociocultural, socioeconomic, and socioenvironmental constraints that have a significant impact on their literacy and living outside school. Indeed, as Edmondson and Shannon (1998) argued, to help the poor in the 21st century, literacy educators and researchers can no longer take refuge in the belief that their job is to teach students to read and hope for the best; rather, they must encourage the development of students' sociological imaginations about their lived realities and reinvigorate efforts to embrace literacy education with struggles for cultural recognition to transcend these realities. That is, they must engage students in literacy activities by which they learn to recognize and rewrite the larger social forces that affect their lives. To do so, literacy educators must extend their efforts beyond the four walls of classrooms and schools to address the limit situations outside schools that constantly impede students' learning inside the classroom. This can be achieved through improving students' social environments and implementing pedagogical practices that link students' learning inside school with their lived realities outside school. For example, teachers can use reports about drug use and violence from the local newspapers as texts for reading and writing instruction. They can design reading and writing activities that involve more interaction and dialogue among students of different cultural, ethnic, or social class backgrounds. They can also involve students in writing commentaries or opinion papers about their ideas to solve these problems and improve the social environment.

Also needed are efforts to change the power relationships between school and home. Li (2006) posited that, to alter the existing power structure and to meet the educational needs of minority families, change must occur reciprocally between school and home, between teachers and parents. For this reciprocal change, efforts must be made in two other critical areas. One area is culture work within the school system to reinvent the literacy curriculum, which is void of multicultural substance. I propose here a culture pedagogy that aims to redesign school literacy practices to enable students to become successful border-crossers who "engage the multiple references that constitute different cultural codes, experiences, and languages" (Giroux, 2005, p. 21). In this pedagogical practice, teachers and educators first need to know about students' lived realties and the sociocultural contexts of their learning in and out of school. For the inner city teachers and educators who often live in the suburbs or outside of the communities in which they teach, getting in touch with students' literacy and living is of critical importance. Li (2006) suggested that teachers must take a culturally reciprocal approach in minority education by which teachers and families mutually learn one another's cultural knowledge. To be culturally reciprocal, teachers and educators must "find effective ways to collect student social and cultural data outside school as we cannot teach when we do not know who we are teaching" (Li, 2006, p. 211). In effect, direct contact with and systematic study of students' families and communities should "become the basis for curriculum planning and instruction, rather than unfounded generalizations or unconfirmed information" (Mercado, 2005, p. 147). This data collection process will not only help teachers recognize the cultural differences between home and school but also enable them to help students understand the discursive discourses and elements surrounding their own lives. Only when teachers come to a deep and comprehensive understanding of school and home cultural practices can they help minority students arrive at a cultural recognition of their social realities. And only by doing so can teachers establish positive relationships with their students and really *care for* them.

Teachers' familiarity with students' out-of-school lived realities will help them redesign school literacy practices and avoid fracturing minority students' literacy experiences. For example, the literacy and living of the three families in this study suggest that teachers must abandon the scripted, one-size-fits-all curriculum to address the diverse levels of literacy fracturing in minority families. Teachers and schools must value students' first languages and cultures and treat them as "funds of knowledge." In fact, National Reading Panel reviews of second-language research concluded that children's literacy learning in their first language is beneficial to their second-language learning (August & Shanahan, 2006). Therefore, having first-language support in school, written and/or oral, will de-fracture students' literacy experiences and successfully involve parents, especially those who are not proficient in English, in the process of educating their children. Mercado (2005) believes that, with the cultural knowledge of their minority students, teachers will be able to "build on and support bilingualism, multidialectalism, biliteracy, and language play for learning in the school" (p. 147). At the very least, teachers will be able to assign students to the right services. For example, if teachers have basic information about the language and literacy backgrounds of Sudanese children, they could help these students find support in Dinka instead of assigning them to an Arabic-speaking teacher.

In terms of literacy instruction, teachers will also be able to individualize the curriculum by addressing different kinds of literacy fracturing. For example, with refugee families who have different cultural and pedagogical traditions and different levels of English proficiency, teachers must use a variety of methods and materials. For this, they need to provide explicit and scaffolded instruction that clearly sets the goals, tasks, reading texts, and learning processes synchronized with students' proficiency levels, learning styles, and special needs (e.g., for students like Fred who is an English language learner with learning disabilities). The school may need to set up some transitional classes for these immigrant children instead of mainstreaming them upon their arrival into age-level classes. For native-born White children such as Scott and Rod, individualized literacy instruction means that they need to be allowed to read from an aesthetic stance that goes beyond filling out worksheets and answering text-based questions. In terms of the writing curriculum, students must be encouraged to make connections with their personal experiences and their cultural backgrounds.

Another important part of the culture pedagogy is to help students recognize the cultural contestations and mismatches in their lives and learn how to reconcile them. González (2005) argued that the school site should provide students with an ideological space not only for the development of bilingualism and biliteracy but also for multidiscursive practices and readings of the world. This means that students need to read not only the direct environment, such as their family and community milieus, but also the world beyond it, such as the dominant society, in which their existence is "either ideologically disparaged or ruthlessly denied" (Giroux, 2005, p. 25). Teachers can help students to read their own worlds by engaging them in "analyzing how ideologies are actually taken up in the contradictory voices and lived experiences of students as they give meaning to the dreams, desires, and subject positions that they inhabit" (p. 24). To do so, teachers must use students' cultures and literacies as texts in literacy education. This means literacy teaching must be built upon students' histories, languages, memories, and community narratives, which are raced and classed. Furthermore, as Giroux argued, literacy education must also allow space for cultural remapping. That is, students not only need to learn how to analyze their lived cultural experiences but also need to develop abilities to explore alternatives that may rewrite their learning trajectories—from those in the margin and prescribed as failures to those in the center with promises for academic success. Only when they develop these abilities can they achieve the true sense of cultural reconciliation.

In conclusion, to help eliminate the negative impact of various sociocultural, socioenvironmental, and socioeconomic factors on minority children's literacy learning in school and at home, teachers and educators, along with various community members and policymakers, must devote their efforts toward improving the physical environment in and out of school. In addition, they must practice a culture pedagogy that bridges school and home cultures and helps students become competent cultural agents who can successfully navigate the complex terrains of race and class relations in their lives while achieving academic success in school.

REFERENCES

August, D., & Shanahan, T. (2006). *Developing literacy in second-language learners: Report of the National Literacy Panel on language-minority children and youth.* Mahwah, NJ: Erlbaum.

Bourdieu, P. (1977). Cultural preproduction and social reproduction. In J. Karabel & A. H. Halsey (Eds.), *Power and ideology in education* (pp. 487–511). New York, NY: Oxford University Press.

Collins, J., & Blot, R. K. (2003). *Literacy and literacies: Text, power, and identity.* Cambridge, England: Cambridge University Press.

Compton-Lilly, C. (2002). *Reading families: The literate lives of urban children.* New York, NY: Teachers College Press.

Creswell, J. W. (2005). *Educational research: Planning, conducting, and evaluating quantitative and qualitative research* (2nd ed.). Columbus, OH: Pearson.

Edmondson, J., & Shannon, P. (1998). Reading education and poverty: Questioning the reading success equation. *Peabody Journal of Education, 73*(3&4), 104–126.

Farr, M. (1994). En los dos idiomas: Literacy practices among Chicago Mexicanos. In B. Moss (Ed.), *Literacy across communities* (pp. 9–47). Cresskill, NJ: Hampton.

Fisher, M. A., & Adler, C. W. (2001). Early reading programs in high-poverty schools: A case study of beating the odds. *The Reading Teacher, 54,* 616–619.

Fordham, S. (1996). *Blacked out: Dilemmas of race, identity, and success at Capital High.* Chicago, IL: University of Chicago Press.

Foucault, M. (1972). *The archeology of knowledge.* New York, NY: Pantheon.

Foucault, M. (1978). *The history of sexuality: Volume I* (R. Hurley, Trans.). New York, NY: Vintage.

Freire, P. (1970). *Pedagogy of the oppressed.* New York, NY: Seabury.

Fuligni, A. J., & Yoshikawa, H. (2003). Socioeconomic resources, parenting, poverty, and child development among immigrant families. In M. H. Bornstein & R. H. Bradley (Eds.), *Socioeconomic status, parenting, and child development* (pp. 107–124). Mahwah, NJ: Erlbaum.

Gee, J. P. (1989). Literacy, discourse, and linguistics: Introduction. *Journal of Education, 171*(1), 5–17.

Gee, J. P. (1991). What is literacy? In C. Mitchell & K. Weiler (Eds.), *Rewriting literacy: Culture and the discourse of the other* (pp. 3–11). New York, NY: Bergin & Garvey.

Giroux, H. (2005). *Border crossing: Cultural workers and the politics of education* (2nd ed.). New York, NY: Routledge.

Glaser, B., & Strauss, A. (1967). *The discovery of grounded theory: Strategies for qualitative research.* Chicago, IL: Aldine.

González, N. (2005). Beyond culture: The hybridity of funds of knowledge. In N. González, L. C. Moll, & C. Amanti (Eds.), *Funds of knowledge: Theorizing practices in households, communities, and classrooms* (pp. 29–46). Mahwah, NJ: Erlbaum.

Hicks, D. (2002). *Reading lives: Working-class children and literacy learning.* New York, NY: Teachers College Press.

Iceland, J., & Scopilliti, M. (2008). Immigrant residential segregation in U.S. metropolitan areas, 1990–2000. *Demography, 45*(1), 79–94.

Izumi, L. T. (2002). *They have overcome: High poverty, high performing schools in California.* San Francisco, CA: Pacific Research Institute for Public Policy.

Kainz, K., & Vernon-Feagans, L. (2007). The ecology of early reading development for children in poverty. *The Elementary School Journal, 107*, 407–427.

Knapp, M. S., & Woolverton, S. (2004). Social class and schooling. In J. A. Banks & C. A. M. Banks (Eds.), *Handbook of research on multicultural education* (2nd ed., pp. 656–681). San Francisco, CA: Jossey-Bass.

Kozol, J. (2004). *The shame of a nation.* New York, NY: Crown.

Lam, W. S. E. (2004). Second language socialization in a bilingual chat room: Global and local considerations. *Language Learning & Technology, 8*(3), 44–65.

Lareau, A. (2003). *Unequal childhoods: Class, race, and family life.* Berkeley: University of California Press.

Lee, E. V., & Burkam, D. T. (2002). *Inequality at the starting gate: Social background differences in achievement as children begin school.* Washington, DC: Economic Policy Institute.

Li, G. (2005). *Asian-American education across the class line: A multi-site report.* Buffalo, NY: GSE, State University of New York Press.

Li, G. (2006). *Culturally contested pedagogy: Battles of literacy and schooling between mainstream teachers and Asian immigrant parents.* Albany: State University of New York Press.

Li, G. (2007). Home environment and second language acquisition: The importance of family capital. *British Journal of Sociology of Education, 28*(3), 285–299.

Li, G. (2008). *Culturally contested literacies: America's "rainbow underclass" and urban schools.* New York, NY: Routledge.

Lincoln, Y. S., & Guba, G. E. (1985). *Naturalist inquiry.* Beverly Hills, CA: Sage.

McBrien, J. L. (2005). Educational needs and barriers for refugee students in the United States: A review of literature. *Review of Educational Research, 75*, 329–364.

Mercado, M. (2005). Seeing what's there: Language and literacy funds of knowledge in New York Puerto Rican homes. In A. C. Zentella (Ed.), *Building on strength: Language and literacy in Latino families and communities* (pp. 134–147). New York, NY: Teachers College Press.

Merriam, S. B. (1998). *Qualitative research and case study applications in education.* San Francisco, CA: Jossey-Bass.

National Assessment of Educational Progress. (2007). *The nation's report card.* Retrieved from http://nationsreportcard.gov/

Ochs, E. (1986). *Culture and language acquisition: Acquiring communicative competence in a Western Samoan village.* New York, NY: Cambridge University Press.

Olsen, L. (1997). *Made in America: Immigrant students in our public schools.* New York, NY: New Press.

Orfield, G., & Lee, C. (2005). *Why segregation matters: Poverty and educational inequality.* Cambridge, MA: The Civil Rights Project at Harvard University.

Perry, P. (2002). *Shades of white: White kids and racial identities in high school.* Durham, NC: Duke University Press.

Portes, A., & Rumbaut, R. G. (1996). *Immigrant America: A portrait* (2nd ed.). Berkeley: University of California Press.

Portes, A., & Rumbaut, R. (2001). *Legacies: The story of the immigrant second generation*. Berkeley: University of California Press.

Portes, A., & Zhou, M. (1993). The new second generation: Segmented assimilation and its variants. *Annals of the American Academy of Political and Social Science, 530*, 74–82.

Purcell-Gates, V. (1996). Stories, coupons and *TV Guide*: Relationship between home literacy experiences and emergent literacy knowledge. *Reading Research Quarterly, 31*, 406–428.

Reese, L. (2009). Literacy practices among immigrant Latino families. In G. Li (Ed.), *Multicultural families, home literacies, and mainstream schooling* (pp. 129–149). Greenwich, CT: Information Age.

Rogers, R. (2003). *A critical discourse analysis of family literacy practices: Power in and out of print*. Mahwah, NJ: Erlbaum.

Rosenblatt, L. M. (2004). The transactional theory of reading and writing. In R. B. Ruddell & N. J. Unrau (Eds.), *Theoretical models and processes of reading* (pp. 1363–1398). Newark, DE: International Reading Association.

Sampson, W. A. (2003). *Poor Latino families and school preparation: Are they doing the right things?* Lanham, MD: Scarecrow.

Schieffelin, B. B., & Ochs, E. (1986). Language socialization. *Annual Review of Anthropology, 15*, 163–191.

Shannon, P. (1998). *Reading poverty*. Portsmouth, NH: Heinemann.

Suárez-Orozco, C., & Suárez-Orozco, M. M. (2001). *Children of immigrants*. Cambridge, MA: Harvard University Press.

Taylor, B. M., Pearson, P. D., Peterson, D. S., & Rodriguez, M. C. (2003). Reading growth in high-poverty classrooms: The influence of teacher practices that encourage cognitive engagement in literacy learning. *The Elementary School Journal, 104*, 3–28.

Thomas, V. (2006, July 16). West Side becomes war zone. *Buffalo News, 2*.

U.S. Census Bureau. (2000). Washington, DC: U.S. Government Printing Office.

Vélez-Ibáñez, C., & Greenberg, J. (2005). Formation and transformation of funds of knowledge. In N. González, L. C. Moll, & C. Amanti (Eds.), *Funds of knowledge: Theorizing practices in households, communities, and classrooms* (pp. 47–71). Mahwah, NJ: Erlbaum.

Wamba, N. G. (2010/this issue). Poverty and literacy: An introduction. *Reading & Writing Quarterly: Overcoming Learning Difficulties, 26*, 109–114.

Responding to the Needs of the Whole Child: A Case Study of a High-Performing Elementary School for Immigrant Children

MARGARY MARTIN
EDWARD FERGUS
PEDRO NOGUERA

New York University, New York, New York, USA

Changes in the demography of the nation's public schools are occurring at a dramatic pace. In states such as California, Texas, and Florida, new immigrants comprise more than a third of the student population. In major cities such as New York, Miami, and Los Angeles, they comprise more than 40% of the student population. Similar changes are occurring in small towns and rural areas throughout the country. This article examines (a) how Washington Elementary, a suburban school, has responded to these dramatic demographic changes; and (b) why this particular school has produced dramatic academic success among immigrant students when so many other suburban schools have not. This article focuses on understanding the school's practices and their implications for literacy achievement. It focuses on whether the interaction between organizational and programmatic practices and the implementation of these reform practices produced a transformative effect upon the school and student learning.

Children of recent immigrants constitute the fastest growing population among school-age children in the United States, and all indictors suggest that their numbers will continue to grow (National Center for Education Statistics, 2007). The imbalance in wealth between the nations of North and South America, the persistent demand of the U.S. economy for cheap labor, and the desperate conditions in many of the villages and towns in Mexico and Central America are all factors that contribute to the continued influx of immigrants (Lovato, 2008; Smith & Malkin, 1997; Suarez-Orozco & Suarez-Orozco, 2008). To a large degree these immigrants will come for the same reasons that Irish, Italian, German, Polish, and other immigrants came to the United States years before—because they perceive this country as a land of opportunity and a place where they can better their lives.

As immigrants continue to come to the United States in large numbers, many of their children will end up in the nation's public schools. As has been true for every other generation of immigrants, it will be left to the public schools to figure out how to absorb, acculturate, and educate immigrant children (Fass, 2007). Changes in the demographic makeup of the nation's public schools are already occurring at a dramatic pace. In states such as California, Texas, and Florida, new immigrants make up more than a third of the student population (Ruiz-de-Valasco, Fix, & Clewell, 2001). In major cities such as New York, Miami, and Los Angeles, they comprise more than 40% of the student population (Kohler & Lazarin, 2007). Similar changes are occurring in small towns and rural areas throughout the United States. This article examines how one suburban school, Washington Elementary,[1] has responded to the dramatic demographic changes that are occurring as a result of immigration and explores why this particular school has been so successful at producing academic success among its immigrant students when so many other suburban schools have not. Over a 10-year period (1997–2007), Washington Elementary transformed into a full-service community school. Moreover, the percentage of students achieving proficiency in fourth-grade English language arts (ELA) rose from 19% in 1998–1999 to 84% in 2000–2001, and 98% attained proficiency in 2005–2006. This examination focuses on understanding the practices of this school and their implications for literacy achievement. This article focuses on whether the interaction between organizational and programmatic practices and the implementation of these reform practices produced a transformative effect upon the school and, consequently, student learning. To better understand how these reforms have worked together to improve students' education, the researchers decided to conduct an exploratory research study using a case study approach premised on the following research questions:

- How has the community school approach operated at Washington Elementary?
- How, if at all, have these community school components interacted to support and sustain language and literacy development among immigrant students?

---

[1]The name of the school has been changed for the purpose of this article.

The researchers explored these questions over a 2-year period (2005–2007) via interviews, focus groups, examination of school archival documents, and analysis of student achievement data.

THEORETICAL FRAMEWORK

To better understand how certain approaches to school reform may directly and indirectly interact with literacy development, the researchers use the case of one exemplary school. They borrow from Uri Bronfenbrenner's (1979) human ecology theory, also known as ecological system theory, to explore how this school and some others manage to succeed when so many others fail. Heavily influenced by the theories of Vygotsky, Bronfenbrenner's theory views a child's development as occurring within a system of relationships that shape his or her environment. Bronfenbrenner's theory describes the ways in which complex "layers" of the environment interact, each having an effect upon a child's development. In his work, Bronfenbrenner described four types of nested environmental systems that influence a child's development: (a) the microsystem of social relationships, which as direct and immediate influences upon a child (e.g., the family, neighbors, or peer group); (b) the mesosystem, which creates a local context and sets the parameters under which the microsystems are operative (e.g., home–school, family–neighborhood); (c) the exosystem, which refers to the physical and economic environment that can influence development indirectly; and (d) the macrosystem, which, at the outermost layer, is the larger cultural and political context that also impacts child development even if its influences are the most indirect (e.g., laws, demographic patterns, economic trends).

In the context of schools, the microsystem can be viewed as the classroom in which the child directly learns to read and write and the practices used by teachers to facilitate learning. Since the enactment of the No Child Left Behind Act of 2001 (NCLB) and the U.S. Department of Education's emphasis on research-based practices, the functioning of the microsystem at the level of the classroom has received considerable attention, typically in the form of "best practice" intervention studies. In an effort to improve reading skills among young children, the U.S. Department of Education has advocated the implementation of rigidly prescribed literacy programs that rely upon standardized curricula for the purpose of cultivating distinct skills that can be tested and monitored over time.

Under NCLB, the mesosystem has also been targeted through reforms aimed at increasing school accountability. With its annual reporting requirements, NCLB compels schools to demonstrate evidence that students are meeting performance standards and imposes penalties upon schools in which insufficient progress has been made. Although this approach to school-level accountability has significantly increased the pressure on schools to produce evidence of student achievement, it has not been successful at addressing the challenges of chronically underperforming schools, in which poor and immigrant children are in many cases disproportionately concentrated (Noguera, 2003). In many of these schools, multiple reforms have been implemented at the same time (e.g., changes in curriculum and professional development for teachers), but relatively little time has been spent evaluating past reforms or looking at how changes that are implemented should interact to improve a child's education. Research on school reform has shown that in order for changes in the operation of schools to work in the best interest of children, careful planning, training, and evaluation are essential (Elmore, Abelmann, & Fuhrman, 1996). Too often, under the pressure to raise tests scores quickly, schools find themselves unable to take the time to make sure that even the most sensible reforms are implemented correctly.

Although it could be argued that NCLB has had an impact at the micro- and mesolevels that impact student achievement directly—even if results have been mixed at best—few could argue that it has addressed the exo- or macrosystems at all. Numerous researchers have shown that concentrated poverty and the social isolation of the poor, two phenomena that are endemic to most urban and many rural areas in the United States, have had a tremendous effect upon the education and well-being of children (Coleman et al., 1966; Rothstein, 1994, 2002; Wilson, 1989, 1997). Similarly, de-industrialization, suburbanization, and the globalization of the world economy have also shaped the quality of life and prospects for economic and social well-being in communities throughout the United States. Such trends also have had an impact upon schools that rely heavily upon local property taxes for resources and the children and families they serve, who in many cases find themselves unable to benefit from the prosperity generated by the "new economy." There is substantial evidence that context at the local, regional, national, and international level matters, and any educational policy that ignores how trends operating at these levels impact classrooms and schools is a policy that will ultimately fail (Reich, 1992). Overall, community school initiatives are one kind of intervention that seeks to address some of the negative outcomes associated with contextual factors that traditionally exist outside of schools by providing health, well-being, and educational services to students and their families. This begs the question: What are the ways in which these contextual supports are related to achievement outcomes, such as literacy skills?

RESEARCH BACKGROUND

The Community School Approach

Washington Elementary became a community school in the late 1990s. The community school approach—an idea that can be traced back to the early writings of John Dewey—is premised on the notion that the conditions for academic learning must also involve attention to the cognitive, emotional, social, physical, and moral development of children. The current movement of community schools began in the late 1980s when various organizations (e.g., Children's Aid Society, Communities in Schools, Beacon Schools) embarked on a reform strategy aimed at forming concrete relationships between schools and nonprofit service organizations in school districts throughout the country. The initial rationale for these community school partnerships was the recognition that the nutritional, mental health, and physical needs of low-income children are primary developmental issues that impact learning. In most cases, schools cannot respond to this broad array of needs alone (Dryfoos, Quinn, & Barkin, 2005). During the late 1980s and throughout the 1990s, the unmet social needs of poor children were exacerbated by policy changes in the macrosystem (e.g., Welfare to Work, deindustrialization, suburbanization) that had the effect of compounding many of the difficulties facing poor children and their families and overwhelming community and school-based resources. The combination of these trends made it increasingly clear that high-poverty schools were in need of assistance.

The community school approach, sometimes called the full-service school, provides children with access to mental health professionals and other social services that go far beyond the standard Title I social worker or guidance counselor. Many community schools maintain a full-time licensed social worker, and in some community schools, such as the ones operated by the Children's Aid Society, mental health services or wellness centers are staffed by two to four social workers and a part-time psychologist. Community schools also maintain a health professional, such as a nurse practitioner, which allows students to receive their annual physicals and prescriptions onsite at the school. Many community schools provide dental services and even orthodontist services. Practically every community school maintains an extensive extended day program that includes academic enrichment and recreation before and after school and often on Saturdays. In addition, many community schools attempt to extend their services to parents and families by providing adult education classes throughout the school day and in particular in the evening and on weekends. All of these services occur in schools that typically operate 10 to 12 hr per day, 6 or 7 days a week. Although the overall number of community schools remains quite low, there is a continued recognition of the need to address the developmental domains of children (i.e., the cognitive, social, emotional, moral, and physical domains) in the social institution in which these children are most influenced and spend majority of their developing years (Armstrong, 2007).

Serving Children of Immigrants

As immigrant children enroll in the nation's public schools, educators are compelled to figure out how to meet their educational needs, chief among these being the need to learn the English language. Schools that serve large populations of immigrant children are faced with a double challenge: Their students need to learn English and gain literacy skills as quickly as possible, and they must learn content across the academic disciplines. Research on language acquisition has shown that meeting this challenge can be extremely difficult. In addition to developing communicative English language proficiency for students whose first language is not English, there is a need to simultaneously build content literacies for English language learners (Wells, 1994), many of whom also have low cognitive academic language proficiency (CALP) skills (August & Shanahan, 2006; Chamot & O'Malley, 1994; García, Wilkinson, & Ortiz, 1995). In many cases, students may gain sufficient proficiency in the English language to exit an English as a second language (ESL) program after 3 years, but for most students it can take between 5 and 7 years to become fully competent in both communicative and academic discourse (Cummins, 1981).

Furthermore, young children of immigrants face multiple disadvantages that place them at risk for school failure. Several recent studies have reported that 23% of immigrant children younger than 6 years old have one or more undocumented parents (Capps, Fix, Ost, Reardon-Anderson, & Passel, 2004; Takanishi, 2004), placing them in a precarious legal circumstance. The risks facing immigrant children extend well beyond their legal status. Recent research on the status of immigrants has shown that the children of immigrants are more likely to live in two-parent families than children born to nonimmigrant parents (Capps et al., 2004). However, they are also more likely than children whose parents were both born in the United States to live in households with incomes that fall below the poverty level and that lack health insurance and stable housing (Capps et al., 2004; Fix & Zimmermann, 2001; Guendelman, Schauffler, & Pearl, 2001). Immigrant children are also more likely to attend segregated schools and schools that are poorly funded (Orfield & Eaton, 1996). Moreover, 56% of immigrant children come from low-income families compared to 19% of children born to U.S.-born parents (Capps et al., 2004). Children of immigrants are also 50% less likely to receive Temporary Assistance for Needy Families and about twice as likely to be in poor health (Capps et al., 2004; Takanishi, 2004).

Despite these harsh realities, a small number of elementary schools have implemented reforms that address some of the challenges involved with educating immigrant children, and they have achieved remarkable results. In a small but significant number of exceptional schools immigrant children are displaying extraordinary resilience and managing to achieve at high levels despite the obstacles they face (Jerald, 2001). This is true in particular in terms of effective literacy development (see Walpole, Justice, & Invernizzi, 2004). As one of these schools, Washington Elementary exemplifies many of the key components of effective instructional practices. As these components have been well documented, the focus here is more on how these effective strategies are implemented within the context of a community school and the implications for immigrant children in terms of gaining literacy skills.

RESEARCH SETTING

The present case study took place in a township located outside a major metropolitan area in the northeastern United Sates. The town itself is nestled between some of the most affluent suburban communities in the country; however, its population is primarily middle and working class. Formerly an industrial center, the township now exhibits many of the characteristics of economic decline common among Rustbelt urban centers throughout the northeast today. Poverty levels in the township are higher than the national and regional averages, and 15.3% of children younger than the age of 18 live in poverty. Like many suburban/small-town communities across the country, the town has received an unprecedented number of immigrants in recent years, primarily from Latin America (46.2%). The second largest ethnic group is Whites (42.8%), followed by much smaller populations of African Americans (7%) and Asians (2.1%).

More than two fifths (41.4%) of the population in the town is foreign born, 82% of whom come from Latin American countries. Of the foreign born who responded to the 2000 Census, the majority (55.2%) reported speaking a foreign language either in addition to or other than English at home. The town also faces issues of transience. Only 58.6% of its residents resided in the same house from 1995 to 2000, with 23.6% of the town's population moving into the township from outside the county within the same time period (U.S. Bureau of the Census, 2000).

SCHOOL SITE

Although the town is not big, it faces many of the complexities faced by large municipalities. These complexities become even more obvious when one looks at its public schools. George Washington Elementary Community

School is a Title I kindergarten–Grade 5 school with 431 students in the 2005–2006 school year. Although located in a suburban community, it has several key enrollment indicators usually associated with urban schools in segregated areas, and like many urban schools in the United States, the student population does not reflect the population of the larger community (Noguera, 2003). Of the students, 95% are minorities—88% are Latino, 6% Black, 6% White, and 1% Asian. The percentage of students identified as limited English proficient is 48%. Although school records indicate that 67% of the students are eligible for free or reduced lunch, administrators believe that the real number is likely much higher. Large numbers of students at Washington come from families with undocumented parents, and their legal status undoubtedly contributes to an unwillingness to fill out reports, even ones that would qualify their children to receive free lunch. Academically speaking, students at Washington face multiple challenges related to language barriers, acculturation, and the numerous effects of poverty.

Despite its challenges, Washington is, by all accounts, a highly successful school. According to Title I and the state's Department of Education, Washington is a "School in Good Standing" that consistently meets its annual yearly progress goal. In addition, the school has received recognition at both the state and national levels for its accomplishments in reducing the achievement gap and for its remarkable academic turnaround since its principal, Dr. Ramirez, took the helm in the fall of 1996.

Most impressive has been the school's success in improving literacy, which surpasses that of schools that serve more privileged populations of students in the United States. Washington has had particular success in raising the achievement of underperforming students. Although it is only one indicator, performance on the state's standardized ELA exam clearly shows that a remarkable change has occurred. According to annual state school reports, in 1998–1999 only 19% of the students who took the Grade 4 statewide ELA exam reached proficiency or above. Just 2 years later that percentage had increased to 84%, and in the 2005–2006 year 98% of Washington's fourth graders reached proficiency or above.

It was this remarkable turnaround that drew the researchers to study how the school has managed to be so successful at raising the literacy levels of its students, particularly given that most schools across the United States that serve similar populations facing a similar set of challenges typically fail. Given how common it is to encounter articles and news stories lamenting the low academic achievement of Latino students, particularly Latino boys, it is important to look at a school whose Latino students are succeeding academically and in which no gender gap in performance exists. Finally, it is important to note that this elementary school is not a selective school that deliberately screens its students. It is a neighborhood school that takes in all children who live in the surrounding neighborhood regardless of their need, status, or circumstance.

METHODS

The study of this school was divided into two phases of data collection. Phase 1 data collection focused on capturing how Washington Elementary is expected to operate. This involved conducting numerous focus groups with school staff, parents, and students on how the school is expected to operate and how the operation of each school component connects to student academic outcomes. Phase 2 data collection focused on capturing the school in action. This data collection involved conducting formal classroom observations, interviews, and focus groups and collecting achievement data over a school year.

Phase 1: How Has the Community School Approach Operated at Washington Elementary?

Washington Elementary took a school-wide, comprehensive approach to all of its reform efforts when it embraced the community school approach in 1997. The research team determined that the best way to capture the school's model was to use a theory of change approach (Weiss, 1998) in the case study research design (Yin, 2002). Theory of change is a process that allows for the explication of how a complex initiative was operationalized to achieve goals that were set. The researchers used theory of change to illustrate the multiple components of a system and the underlying assumptions that guided implementation of school change plans and that were expected to work in concert to achieve desired outcomes. Theory of change provides the opportunity to know not only what the reforms were expected to achieve but also how they were expected to achieve it (Weiss, 1998). During the course of the research the researchers found this method to be particularly effective in allowing them to untangle the specific reforms implemented, the goals of the school's community reforms, and how each component was expected to address student needs. In addition, the approach allowed the researchers to model the intricate and overlapping connections across school reforms.

In the first phase of the research at the school (2004–2005), the researchers conducted a series of open-ended interviews and focus groups with multiple stakeholders, including school leadership (i.e., principal, community school director, and parent liaison), teachers and staff, and school partners (i.e., nurse, social worker, and dentist), to understand the school's theory of change. Three focus groups were conducted with school leadership, teaching staff, and school partners. The focus group protocols maintained four constructs tied to building the theory of change: (a) overall goals of the implemented reforms, (b) long-term and short-term outcomes related to the overarching goals, (c) practices and programs resulting in outcomes, and (d) the theoretical purpose of the practices and programs. Each focus group was asked questions representing each of these constructs in order to identify the "outcome to practice to theory" schematic practitioners across Washington created about the community school approach. Once the theory of change had been conceptualized, the next step was to document the system in action.

Phase 2: How, if at All, Have These Community School Components Interacted to Support and Sustain Language and Literacy Development Among Immigrant Students?

To capture the system in action (2005–2007), the researchers collected data over a 2-year period from multiple data sources in relation to the theory of change outcomes, practices, and theory outlined in Phase 1 of the study. This data collection occurred in three waves during the 2005–2006 school year and two waves in the 2006–2007 school year. The researchers conducted 10 focus groups and formal and informal interviews with school leadership, staff, and school partners. The focus group and interview protocols contained open-ended and close-ended questions regarding the following constructs: practice/program operation, student–teacher interactions, teacher–teacher interactions, teacher pedagogical concepts (i.e., what is teaching and how does a teacher deliver content), professional development practice, and social service delivery. The researchers also conducted participant observations of school activities and ethnographic classroom observations in three waves in 2005–2006 and 2006–2007. They conducted participant observations of social service program delivery, student–teacher interactions, teacher–teacher interactions, staff meetings and retreats, and professional development activities. Finally, the researchers collected artifacts such as annual school reports going back 10 years, school program events, and district policy and other school documents during the course of the 2 years.

Data Analysis

Qualitative data from the focus groups, interviews, and observations were analyzed using conceptually clustered matrices and within-case and across-case qualitative analysis (Miles & Huberman, 1994) for each of community service initiative—educational services, health and mental well-being services, and professional development services. After reading source data, the researchers open-coded data and then developed conceptually clustered matrices of categories that appeared to represent connections within and across the community domains. These categories were used to conduct deductive analysis within a data matrix that allowed for within-case and across-case analysis. The data were then examined in relation to the theory of change, and a conceptual model was created to capture the connections of each community of practice to the others. Analytical memos were used throughout the coding process in order to reinspect the data, modify predetermined codes, and construct new codes (Miles & Huberman, 1994). This coding and analysis process encouraged deductive as well as inductive coding and interpretation throughout the analysis. In order to highlight the connections that emerged across the communities of practice in relation to educational development, the findings describe a simplified version of the model with only the aspects of the network of professional practice conceptual model.

FINDINGS

The Theory of Change: Building Community Partnerships

In both formal and informal interviews, whenever the adults at the school were questioned about why they used a particular practice they repeated the mantra "To meet the needs of the whole child." This goal guided the theory of change used at the school. However, complicating the challenges faced by Washington Elementary School in its efforts to address the needs of the whole child is the lack of resources it has to implement reforms that were deemed necessary in light of student needs. For example, school administrators realized that if the school were to meet the educational needs of students it would also have to respond to some of their health needs. Forging partnerships with community agencies and community-based organizations (CBOs) was essential to enacting this change. These partnerships were created to address two primary areas: the learning needs of the child (and by extension the learning needs of the school's teachers) and the health and social needs of the child. Within these two domains, three areas were targeted in the school's efforts that together contributed to the school's success: creating the community school to provide community health and social services to students and their families, providing extended learning opportunities for enrichment and remediation through the school's after-school and summer programs, and improving academic programs through targeted professional development and teacher induction to improve teacher quality through onsite school–university partnerships.

As a result of the resourcefulness and creativity of the staff and administration, Washington provides its students and their families with a broad array of social services made possible through a multitude of partnerships with the local community. The school has a health clinic that offers dental, mental health, and medical services to the children in the school. It offers an adult ESL evening program, and it provides a number of extended day programs that provide enrichment activities for the children. In addition, the school maintains "Washington Family Services," which is focused on "building community from the outside in" (from school documents), engaging parents as learners through various topical workshops (e.g., Every Person Influences Children training) and formal social gatherings (e.g., parent–teacher association, second cup of coffee). Washington works closely with CBOs that provide some of the mental health and dental services as well as connect Washington to other networks of resources for parents (e.g., Habitat for Humanity, adult education programs at local community colleges).

Although the services provided by Washington are intended to address the immediate and social needs of students and parents, the school's leadership reported that it is well aware that such an approach is not enough to improve academic performance. Washington has developed a coherent strategy for meeting the academic needs of its students and has aligned to the developmental goals of a community school. Cognizant of the fact that many of the immigrant children served by the school lack formal literacy in their native language and come from homes with a limited ability to provide appropriate academic reinforcement, the school has undertaken a variety of strategies to respond to the literacy needs of its students.

IMPROVING LITERACY THROUGH EXTENDED LEARNING OPPORTUNITIES

To meet accountability standards under NCLB, schools are under pressure to improve student performance on standardized tests. In low-income areas, many schools respond to this pressure by narrowing the curriculum and eliminating recreation and enrichment opportunities. However, such remediation efforts that emphasize test preparation rarely succeed in sustaining increases in student achievement (Eaton, 2007). Given that children between the ages of 5 and 14 spend 60% to 80% of their time out of school (Coltin, 1999), research suggests that more emphasis should be placed on meeting the academic needs of children by developing extended day programs (Halpern, 1999). Too often, the families that need after-school care for their elementary school children must rely upon substandard programs whose focus is more on supervision than enrichment (Shumow, 2001).

To meet the unique academic, health, and social needs of its primarily newcomer student population, Washington Elementary's day program is organized around the following integrated focuses: developing language and literacy, instilling character and promoting caring, experiential learning, and teamwork. In general, English acquisition programs (e.g., bilingual education and ESL) focus primarily on the acquisition of English language proficiency, especially in the elementary grades, with only limited attention given to academic English acquisition in content areas (August & Hakuta, 1997; Chamot & O'Malley, 1994; Lee & Fradd, 1998). At Washington, however, both English language proficiency and CALP development are central to the school's day program. The school also works on building students' problem-solving skills by developing students' social language. The school infuses social language development into its character education program, turning conflict mediation, classroom meetings, and parties into opportunities to improve problem-solving skills while simultaneously developing English literacy skills. The school also hosts a wide variety of extended day learning opportunities in which literacy development is fostered among students through district-wide initiatives and local partnerships.

Washington Elementary provides a rich array of both extended day and summer programs to enrich the education of its children. With funding from the 21st Century Community Learning Center program, the school has been able to sponsor an extensive tutoring and summer learning program administered by a local university partner. This allows the school to offer a wide variety of individualized learning opportunities for students that reinforce and compliment literacy strategies that are used during the school day. These extended day programs are extremely popular, and parental support has been widespread. However, as is true across the nation, demand has outpaced available spaces (Hall, Yohalem, Tolman, & Wilson, 2003; Halpern, 1999; Hofferth & Jankuniene, 2001), and there is a long waiting list of prospective students.

Extracurricular and academic enrichment programs are tightly aligned to the academic program Washington offers during the school day. Language and literacy development is at the center of the school's academic focus during the day, and programs that support and enrich literacy are also the central focuses of the extended day program. The programs offered include an enrichment program for advanced students; a theater arts program; homework help; as well as classes in arts and crafts, chess, and technology. Under the supervision of Dr. Perondi, students in the university partner's preservice teacher education program implement a theme-based academic enrichment summer program and an after-school reading practicum that provides one-on-one remediation during the school year. In preparation for statewide exams that begin in the fourth grade, students receive individualized instruction in their specific areas of need, such as writing essays or following directions. Though the school's emphasis is on a comprehensive approach to meeting student needs, teachers and administrators attribute the school's superior performance in part to the test prep program.

The day program also emphasizes character education, experiential learning, and team building. These elements are also central to the extended day programs. The "We Care" program led by a CBO offers extracurricular programs in social skills, recreational sports and tennis, dance, music, and nutrition as well as remediation in the form of homework support and enrichment through technology and chess.

Given the multiple partnerships and programs involved in community school extended day initiatives, sustaining these relationships and diverse programs is a complicated endeavor (Dryfoos, 1999). The network of professional practice at Washington has created a mechanism to facilitate, adapt, and sustain the partnerships through regular articulation of the shared mission and goals. Research has shown that when such alliances can be sustained they are more likely to produce improved school outcomes and an improved school climate; greater student engagement, motivation, and efficacy; and an increased ability to connect families (Dryfoos, 1999; Epstein et al., 2002). It must be pointed out that although the network of professional practice has been able to ensure the quality and alignment of the extended programs to ensure they meet the school's goals for its students, instability in securing the resources to sustain these efforts poses a constant threat to the good work at Washington. Although the school leadership and the community advisory committee have been relentless in their efforts to secure new funding sources, the lack of financial stability could undermine this important work.

ONSITE PROFESSIONAL DEVELOPMENT AND TEACHER INDUCTION

It is well accepted that professional development is key to improving teacher quality in schools. Successful professional development programs include such important elements as teacher collaboration, ongoing long-term support, resources and materials, and open communication with the local school staff (Klingner, 2004). In recent years, some attention has been focused on site-based professional development and teacher induction. Research suggests that there are many benefits to site-based professional development, such as in terms of fostering teacher leadership, creating a means to establish a shared knowledge base and common practices, and strengthening the induction of new teachers (Bloom & Stein, 2004; Boone, Hartzman, & Mero, 2006; Crowther, 1998; Danielson, 2002; Gebhard, 1998). For in-service teachers, onsite professional development can be designed to reduce some of the difficulties that typically confront new teachers (Anderson, Smith, & Peasely, 2000) by providing the opportunity to learn about practice in a real classroom setting with the support of experienced teachers (McDermott, Gormley, Rotherberg, & Hammer, 1995).

Washington Elementary has a number of professional development initiatives in place at its school. These initiatives include a school-wide initiative to build a "professional learning community" facilitated by an outside consultant and aimed at improving language and literacy instruction, character education training, curriculum and technology, and integration training. The school has also developed a partnership with a local private liberal arts college located in a nearby town to collaborate on a number of teacher preparation and professional development endeavors, including establishing a professional development school for the school district on site at the school. Through this collaboration, they have developed onsite graduate teacher preparation courses and student teacher field placements, an ESL teacher institute, a new teacher induction program, and an onsite literacy demonstration lab. Teachers at all levels of development receive support from their colleagues, their mentors, the principal, and university partners/instructors that is embedded in the daily context of the live classroom and that marries method to content.

A Network of Professional Practice

> You can't survive in a place like this if you didn't really care about kids. I think you'd have a hard time working here if you didn't genuinely like kids because you wouldn't let your kids go to the nurse. (Teacher)

Although each initiative was implemented to meet the needs of the immigrant population in the school, the initial data analyses revealed a sort of *network of professional practice* that facilitates the absorption of these areas of services. It is hypothesized that this network makes it possible for the school to shape the contours of the ecological context of the children it serves and its interaction within the school space. The school-wide initiatives described previously have been instrumental in the development of three concrete yet overlapping support mechanisms that form the anchors of the school's sustained reform. Each of these anchors serves students directly and indirectly through their connections to one another.

These support mechanisms appear to function similarly to Lave and Wenger's (1991) concept of a community of practice. *Communities of practice* have been defined as "groups of people who share a concern or a passion for something they do and learn how to do it better as they interact" (Wenger, 2006). Being in the same class, team, or school is not enough to create a community of practice; rather, being a community of practice, according to Wenger, requires the presence of the following three characteristics: (a) the domain—or identity defined by a shared common interest, implying a shared commitment and competence around the area of interest; (b) the community—or shared engagement in activities around the common interest; and (c) shared practice—or the development of shared resources in the forms of tools and experiences and interactions to solve problems. Lave and Wenger's concept has often been applied to the practices of schooling, including work around creating "professional learning communities" in schools, in which teachers take shared responsibility for learning, peer mentoring, and shared reflection (Bloom & Stein, 2004; Bryk, Camburn, & Louis, 1999; Hargreaves, 1994; Wenger, 1998).

It could be argued that at Washington, the concept of professional learning communities has been further incorporated into a wider professional network whose overarching goal is to provide for the needs of the whole child. As one teacher succinctly put it, "Every single one of the adults in this building—their job is to deliver." Each community is involved in some aspect of this goal—whether it be a child's physical or academic development, or top-notch teachers, or the needs of the students' parents or families. In addition to the community that exists among teachers and instructional staff, two more communities exist at the school that serve as primary support mechanisms for students and teachers at the school: (a) community services through school-based health and social services centers and (b) the professional development school as part of the school's university partnership.

At the microlevel, each support mechanism has a direct relationship with students. It is posited that it is in the way in which each community within the mesosystem connects to one another, through its web of mutually supporting relationships, that they have created a school that is able to mitigate some of the impact of the eco- and macrosystems. The network of professional practice also provides the conditions in which language and literacy development can be fostered and thrive.

Based on the data collected over 2 years (2005–2007), the researchers identified themes or *structural bonds* that may bind the mesosystem together. Each community within the network, including its goals and the direct services it provides, is briefly described. Then common themes that form the connections or structural bonds across the networks are identified. These bonds are common core values, common language, and common reflective practice. Last, three conditions are discussed that appear to under-gird the system and be vital to the sustenance of the network or professional practice at the school. The findings suggest that these conditions include common physical space, community trust, and leadership.

NETWORK ORGANIZATION

Because the act of daily instruction remains the best predictor of student performance, the child and teacher sit at the center of the model (see Figure 1). All partners provide support to both the students and teachers. As part of Washington Elementary's overarching goal to provide for the needs of the whole child, the school has formed a partnership with the local liberal arts college (university partner). Both the university and community partners also provide direct services to the students, as noted earlier. There are also examples of cross-partner collaboration, for example when one of the CBO parent programs partnered with the university partner to bring parents to the campus of the university to learn about higher education. Although there are additional multiple partnerships with a number of community agencies and CBOs who provide services on site as well as outside professional development and district initiatives, the researchers focus only on the primary partnerships here to demonstrate how these supports are central to the school's ability to enhance students' language and literacy development.

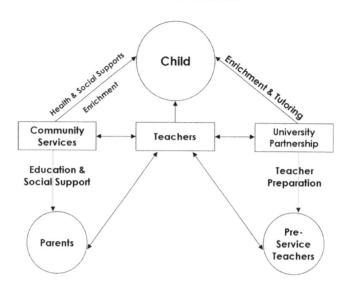

FIGURE 1 Network of professional practice: providing for the needs of the whole child.

In addition to its work with students, the university partnership provides professional development to support teachers and facilitate action research. The CBOs work with individual teachers to address the physical, emotional, and learning needs of individual students and to support classroom practice. Furthermore, the two communities focus their attention on additional constituents of concern, as previously described. For example, as a professional development school, the university partner collaborates with the school provides onsite methods courses and student teacher placements at the school as part of its preservice teaching program. The CBOs are also the primary mechanism serving the families of students in the school, offering ESL instruction to adults and parenting support groups. So, each community in fact has three goals: To serve students, to serve teachers, and—within the traditional domains of teacher education and family services—to serve preservice teachers and parents. Therefore, their goals are specialized but also interrelated, as outlined in Table 1.

Although high-need schools may initiate promising reforms by introducing partnerships to their schools, creating partnerships that function well and that can sustain themselves long enough to impact student success has proven to be a difficult task. The findings indicate three common *structural bonds* that create what a community partner described as "synergy" across the network: the establishment of common values, a common language, and a common reflective practice across the network of professional practice. These bonds are integral to the success of Washington Elementary in supporting its children.

TABLE 1 Goals of Partner Communities of Practice

Goal	University partnership	Community-based organizations
Goal 1: Students	Improve student outcomes through providing enrichment and remediation services to students.	Improve student health and well-being by providing physical, dental, and social services to students. Provide academic support through enrichment and remediation extended day programs.
Goal 2: Teachers	Improve knowledge and pedagogical skills. Provide academic support and guidance to teachers through professional development and academic support services.	Provide academic support to teachers through providing professional development on the health and social needs of the students and their families and working directly with teachers to serve the needs of particular students. Provide support for teacher instruction through enrichment and remediation programs for students.
	Teachers	*Parents*
Goal 3: Traditional constituency	Provide instruction, guidance and support to preservice teachers. Create multiple opportunities for preservice teachers to observe and practice teaching linguistically and culturally diverse students.	Provide health and social service support to parents and families. Provide educational programs for adults and educational support for parents.

Common values. Every morning, along with the Pledge of Allegiance, students in every classroom recite the school's four common core values: respect, responsibility, tolerance, and kindness. These common core values emerged out of the school's Character Education program and serve as the foundational bond of Washington Elementary's school culture. Although originally conceived for the students, there is an expectation that everyone—child or adult—will abide by the common core values.

In interviews, several staff and parents explained that the core values were identified through a consensus-building process that involved the entire school community. After collectively deciding that character education would be a focus of the school's work, "we came together as a faculty and we decided that we were going to have four character ed[ucation] values," explained a teacher. "And there was a debate as to what those four characteristics were going to be. And we came to a consensus and it was respect, responsibility, tolerance, and kindness." Further proof that the core values emerged through consensus rather than being imposed by the principal came from another focus group with the school partners. When asked the question "When Washington children graduate from fifth grade, what do we leave with?" the partners overwhelmingly responded "Internalized core values."

According to the school's Implementation Plan for 2004, these common core values are infused into all aspects of school life and are intended to lead to the "cross-fertilization of ideas and programs in ways that [enhance] learning for all children." In the classroom observations, the researchers saw this "cross-fertilization" at work integrated with literacy activities when students were working with one another independently at literacy stations. For example, on one visit to a second-grade classroom the researchers observed a boy and a girl sitting in front of an oversized book resting against an easel. As the girl used a pointer to identify words in a sentence, the boy read out loud. When he became stuck with words he did not know how to pronounce, the girl patiently prompted the boy to sound them out, smiling and offering words of encouragement at each attempt and congratulations at success. In addition, the school has also set up a buddy system within and across classrooms so that older students can mentor younger students. When discussing the impact of character education on their students, teachers referred to connectedness, ownership, and a "heightened sense of the social needs of their [the students'] community" that they believe have resulted from "sharing common core values" (teacher focus group, April 2007).

Through observations and interviews, the researchers learned that the core values provide staff, parents, and students with a basis for bonding and developing a strong sense of community. As one teacher explained,

I think the kids are also sensitive to knowing that their parents aren't fluent in English, maybe as fluent as they are, so whenever there are these parent committees, conferences, or meetings, they want their parents to be part of it because they can contribute to something like that and maybe learn about what they are learning about but in a comfortable setting. So you'll often see that when they [students] get the notes, [they'll ask] what is this about? Is this for my mom? When is this meeting? What is this about? So that they can kind of relay the message to Mom, "Oh Mom! This is an important note, this is going to be with Florence, why don't you read this note because this is about this, and this is good."

Common language. "We had the Washington mission, where the cores [are] said everyday, which was common language, and it promoted the common culture." "It goes back to common culture and common language." "Academically, there is a common language that they [teachers] use with the [literacy program], so academically there is a common language."

Whether talking about the core values, the school climate, or instruction, members of the Washington community often referred to the school's use of a "common language." In fact, as visitors at the school it was remarkable the similarity of common language heard across the school and observed in classrooms and hallways as different people described the school. From room to room and across grade levels during literacy blocks, the use of common terminology was heard from teachers and students alike. Even during the focus group, community partners—which included university professors, the community health service provider, and a local philanthropist—all used similar language when discussing the school's culture, values, and goals for its students.

This common language for behavior and instruction is expansive, providing a language-rich and language-reliable environment for English language learners. Common language is used in resolving student conflicts, during classroom meetings, on instruction schedules, and in posters around the school and in the classrooms on the codes of conduct and rules for punctuation. Teachers attributed several benefits to children from the use of a common language, including the ability to hold "high-quality conversations" with their peers and adults. Teachers reported that because new language and routines do not need to be retaught from year to year, language reliability enables children to develop social literacy and CALP while simultaneously saving instructional time.

During a focus group with the school staff, the researchers asked how the school was able to develop that common academic language. As it turns out, decisions around language, like those around the core values, were quite intentional. Each year, the school chooses a focus for its professional development. For example, in one year it was a writer's workshop (a process that emphasizes revision through reciprocal editing), in another year it was reading across the curriculum (with an emphasis on nonfiction). Through site-based professional development and coaching, teachers develop lesson plans and incorporate the common language that will be used across the school. This process was first introduced in staff professional development trainings but is now an integral part of the school's staff meetings. "We put together workshops, developing something on chart paper and we all decide—Are we happy with this? Are we going to add anything? And we did it gradually."

Shared language also binds the three communities across the network, serving as a caring safety net for the students. "I think, when we talk about common language, I think the common bond really is—everybody in the room here—we care about kids. That's the common bond." Taken together, common language and core values create the conditions for language development (in terms of English language proficiency, CALP, and social language development) without demeaning children's home languages.

Common reflective practice. "I mean, every meeting we have . . . I don't know if I've met anyone like Linda [the principal]—when she has a meeting there are charts all over the room."

The school improvement plan is a serious document used at the school. Using multiple data sources beyond standardized test scores (attendance, grades, discipline referrals, etc.) and listening to voices from all constituencies, the school determines its needs and goals. School staff work toward improving student achievement by collectively reflecting upon the kinds of assessments and student projects that will develop skills and further academic engagement.

Work samples are systematically collected three times during the year and analyzed and discussed by teachers. In addition to assessing and planning around individual students and student cohorts, staff use these assessments to agree on the focus of the following year's professional development. The academic goal for the first year when the researchers collected data at the school was writing and the use of literacy stations. By the second year, not only were literacy stations an intrinsic part of the school's literacy program, but the concept was further applied to other curricular areas, including music. The researchers observed students seated in the cafeteria at separate tables and at a portable computer learning how to play piano, write musical notations, listen to songs, as well as read and write music.

Across the network, the adults at Washington understand and reflect upon data related to student performance. This is not to maintain a watch over test scores; rather, teachers use data to understand a full range of student needs. For example, they know the percentage of students who are covered by health insurance (more than 90% last year), and the social worker knows exactly how the fourth-grade class performed on the state's ELA exam. The primary vehicle for reflection across the network of professional practice is the annual end-of-the-year faculty retreat. During this retreat, which is held on the campus of the university partner, partners, administrators, teachers, and staff analyze data from the school year. At such meetings the principal shares preliminary data on standardized exams and data on family participation at school events, the health center presents data on the use of its services and shares the accomplishments and goals of the health center, and the school psychologist and social worker report on the services supplied to children and parents. The goal of this exercise is to ensure that the entire staff understands and can assess how well the school is doing in meeting and responding to the needs of the students and families they serve.

NETWORK SUPPORTS

Over time, it became clear that the network could not sustain itself on its own. As the research progressed, the researchers began to focus more on the conditions undergirding the network of professional practice that appeared to sustain the reforms implemented at the school and to contribute to the relative ease with which new initiatives seemed to be absorbed. The research suggests three primary conditions that seemed to be essential to the growth and maintenance of the network: common physical space, community trust, and leadership.

Common physical space. The modifier *onsite* is often attached to terms in the community schools and preservice teacher education literature. By being on site, a community school has easier access to children and families that are often very hard to reach through traditional social service arms, and developing teachers can learn about teaching in an everyday context through guided observation, action research projects, and student teaching under the mentorship of both teachers at the school and their university supervisors. Taken together, services are designed to ensure that new teachers and community service providers understand and share the goals of the school. Certainly, shared space alone does not ensure that these common bonds will emerge among those providing professional services at the school. Rather, it is the shared goals and common vision that are rooted in the core values and the common language that make possible the high level of coordination and cooperation among all parties.

Community trust. The importance of institutional trust, like leadership, is vital to school health (Bryk & Schneider, 2003). Teaching has traditionally been an autonomous task and has often led to a culture of distrust among teachers, administrators, parents, and children. In contrast, the following example highlights how trust exists at many levels at Washington Elementary:

> It's nice for [students] to be able to go to the guidance center and have someone to speak to, and just help them through an issue, that I can't necessarily do as the teacher because I have 20 other kids that [I need] to be able to handle, that I need to be able to accommodate and teach at the time. So, if a child is having a bad day, they may see, well, used to see Luisa [the school psychologist]. Even Laura [the third-grade teacher] has some great relationships with kids, and she's not necessarily a social worker or a psychologist, but she's seen them since third grade or maybe even earlier than that...I just know that they have relationship with Laura and I'll say, "Would you like to [speak to Ms. Delagato]? You may not feel comfortable speaking with me."

In this example several levels of trust at play. First, there is the recognition that as a teacher this woman cannot solve every issue for every child all the time, and this truth is acceptable both to feel and to express to others. Feeling isolated and inadequate is a common response with teachers and can often lead to inaction on behalf of the child. No one person can meet the needs of every child all the time. When teachers place trust in other teachers and professionals, children to receive the help they need. Second, teachers can be quite protective of their students and are often hesitant to entrust others with them. The willingness of teachers, counselors, and administrators to work together to meet the needs of their students serves as another indication of the trust that permeates the school.

Leadership. To create a purposeful professional network made up of professional learning communities is a complex challenge and requires strong leadership both to create meaningful opportunities and to allow these structural bonds to develop across communities and to grow and sustain the network over time.

In order to bring about sustainable education reform, the school leadership needs to be invested in the process. School climate, quality instruction, and student achievement are often attributed to effective school leadership (Akhaven, 2005; Gullatt & Lofton, 1996; Larsen & Malen, 1997; Mendel, Watson, & MacGregor, 2002). At Washington, the school principal was consistently cited as a person who had cultivated collegial staff relationships, kept everyone focused on student success and continuous learning, and involved teachers as decision makers and implementers of school-wide plans (Fleming, 1999). The principal was seen as a person who was open to new ways of operating the school and embracing suggestions from her staff.

Dr. Ramirez regularly participates in staff professional development, learning alongside her staff and even practicing the skills learned in their presence. By keeping abreast of the latest changes in instructional practice the principal is able to evaluate teachers with a clear understanding of their work. Equally important, her participation in professional development helps to create a professional climate in which taking risks is accepted and promoted and accountability is shared at all levels. Dr. Ramirez is widely praised as a leader who has been extremely savvy at securing resources for her students, teachers, and families. As she told the researchers many times, her prerequisite question is always "What do the kids get out of it?"

Complementing her leadership is her partnership with the school's community coordinator. Instead of a vice-principal, the assistant leader is the community coordinator, who is in charge of all community partnerships and initiatives. Almost always seen side by side, the principal and the community coordinator embody the integration of community services and instruction through collaboration on all initiatives to ensure that community and academic partnerships are aligned with the school's vision.

Further evidence of the principal's willingness to share leadership roles at the school can be seen in the critical role performed by another key leader at the school. The school social worker is one of the most highly respected individuals at the school. She runs the parent support group; coteaches parenting courses with the school psychologist; and has worked extensively with individual parents on personal issues of alcoholism, health needs, and domestic violence. She is revered by teachers and parents alike at the school and serves as a central bridge between school staff and parents as well as between families and the health and social services centers.

Leadership is further distributed to team leaders who plan and implement particular professional development initiatives. Teachers who attain skills from an initiative may quickly be paired up with teachers who are having a more difficult time learning the new skill or practice. This form of differentiated professional development with layered mentoring from the leadership down and teacher capacity building through distributed leadership is integral to the school's approach to professional development. This approach extends to the teaching support staff as well. For example, Dr. Ramirez encouraged a teacher's aide who provides bilingual support to enroll in a local university and study to become a teacher. Taken together, shared physical space, community trust, and leadership serve to sustain the network by contributing to the conditions that allow each domain to do its work and allow for common bonds to be formed.

DISCUSSION

Learning From George Washington Elementary Community School

What is important about a school like Washington Elementary is that it reminds one of what is possible. Although children of immigrants throughout the United States are experiencing high rates of academic failure and are dropping out of school in droves (Passel, 2006), schools like Washington show that this need not be the case. By focusing deliberately and consistently upon the needs of the whole child and by carefully constructing a network of professional practice, the school has been able to develop a safe and supportive learning community where children can flourish.

It is important to recognize that at a time when many schools remain narrowly focused upon the microlevel of student–teacher interactions in their efforts to promote student achievement, schools like Washington succeed in part because they have adopted a broader vision. By responding to the needs of the child at the mesolevel through community partnerships that serve students and their families, Washington is able to mitigate some of the hardships that are operative at the exo- and macrolevels, namely poverty, unemployment, racial discrimination, and growing anti-immigrant sentiment.

If schools are to succeed in meeting the needs of immigrant children, such an approach is not merely laudable but essential. Immigrants, particularly the undocumented, are marginalized and increasingly subjected to harassment and hostility. Given that it is highly unlikely that the country will experience a massive exodus of immigrants any time soon (in fact data on influx patterns show the opposite to be true), the sooner policymakers realize that it is in the national interest to integrate immigrants and ensure that they have access to the support and services they need to escape poverty and the low-wage jobs they fill, the better off all of us will be. Realistically, it may take some time before any significant changes are seen in U.S. policy toward immigrants. In the meantime, it will increasingly fall to schools to find ways to help immigrant children to adapt and acquire the skills they will need to succeed in this country. The example of schools like Washington will hopefully show them that this task is indeed possible.

REFERENCES

Akhaven, N. (2005). Creating and sustaining a collaborative culture. *Leadership*, *34*(5), 20–23.

Anderson, L. M., Smith, D. C., & Peasely, K. (2000). Integrating learner and learning concerns: Prospective elementary science teachers' paths and progress. *Teaching and Teacher Education, 16*, 547–574.

Armstrong, T. (2007). The curriculum superhighway. *Educational Leadership*, *64*(8), 16–20.

August, D., & Hakuta, K. (1997). *Improving schooling for language-minority children: A research agenda*. Washington, DC: U.S. Department of Education.

August, D., & Shanahan, T. (2006). *Developing literacy in second-language learners: Report of the National Literacy Panel on Language-Minority Children and Youth*. Mahwah, NJ: Erlbaum.

Bloom, G., & Stein, R. (2004). Building communities of practice. *Leadership*, *34*(1), 20–22.

Boone, E., Hartzman, E., & Mero, D. (2006). A collaborative approach to performance. *Principal Leadership (Middle School Edition)*, *6*(10), 31–34.

Bronfenbrenner, U. (1979). *The ecology of human development*. Cambridge, MA: Harvard University Press.

Bryk, A., Camburn, E., & Louis, K. S. (1999). Professional community in Chicago elementary schools: Facilitating factors and organizational consequences. *Educational Administration Quarterly*, *35*, 751–781.

Bryk, A., & Schneider, B. (2003). Trust in schools: A core resource for school reform. *Educational Leadership*, *60*(6), 40–45.

Capps, R., Fix, M., Ost, J., Reardon-Anderson, J., & Passel, J. S. (2004). *The health and well-being of young children of immigrants*. Washington, DC: Urban Institute.

Chamot, A. U., & O'Malley, J. M. (1994). *The CALLA handbook: Implementing the cognitive academic language learning approach*. Reading, MA: Addison-Wesley.

Coleman, J., Campbell, E. Q., Hobson, C. J., McPartland, J., Mood, A. M., Weinfeld, E. D., & York, R. L. (1966). *Equality and educational opportunity*. Washington, DC: U.S. Government Printing Office.

Coltin, L. (1999). *Enriching children's out-of-school time*. Champaign, IL: ERIC Clearinghouse on Elementary and Early Childhood Education. (ERIC Document Reproduction Service No. ED429737)

Crowther, S. (1998). Secrets of staff development support. *Educational Leadership*, *55*(5), 75–76.

Cummins, J. (1981). Age on arrival and immigrant second language acquisition in Canada: A reassessment. *Applied Linguistics*, *2*, 132–149.

Danielson, C. (2002). *Enhancing professional practice: A framework for teaching*. Alexandria, VA: Association for Supervision and Curriculum Development.

Dryfoos, J. G. (1999). The role of the school in children's out-of-school time. *The Future of Children*, *9*, 117–134.

Dryfoos, J. G., Quinn, J., & Barkin, C. (2005). *Community schools in action: Lessons from a decade of practice*. New York, NY: Oxford University Press.

Eaton, S., & Orfield, G. (2003). Rededication not celebration. *College Board Review*, *200*, 28–33.

Elmore, R., Abelmann, C. H., & Fuhrman, S. H. (1996). The new accountability in state education reform: From process to performance. In H. F. Ladd (Ed.), *Holding schools accountable: Performance-based reform in education* (pp. 65–98). Washington, DC: Brookings Institution.

Epstein, J. L., Sanders, M. G., Simon, B. S., Salinas, K. C., Joanshorn, N. R., & Van Voorhis, F. L. (2002). *School, family and community partnerships: Your handbook for action* (2nd ed.). Thousand Oaks, CA: Corwin.

Fass, P. S. (2007). *Children of a new world: Society, culture, and globalization.* New York, NY: New York University Press.

Fix, M., & Zimmermann, W. (2001). All under one roof: Mixed-status families in an era of reform. *International Migration Review, 35,* 397–419.

Fleming, G. (1999). Principals and teachers: Continuous learners. *Issues...About Change, 7*(2), 1–8.

García, S. B., Wilkinson, C. Y., & Ortiz, A. A. (1995). Enhancing achievement for language minority students: Classroom, school and family contexts. *Education and Urban Society, 27,* 441–462.

Gebhard, M. (1998). A case for professional development schools. *TESOL Quarterly, 32,* 501–510.

Guendelman, S., Schauffler, H. H., & Pearl, M. (2001). Unfriendly shores: How immigrant children fare in the U.S. health system. *Health Affairs, 20,* 257–266.

Gullatt, D., & Lofton, B. (1996). *The principal's role in promoting academic gain.* (ERIC Document Reproduction Service No. ED403227)

Hall, G., Yohalem, N., Tolman, J., & Wilson, A. (2003). *How afterschool programs can most effectively promote positive youth development as a support to academic achievement: A report commissioned by the Boston After-School for All Partnership.* Wellesley, MA: National Institute on Out-of-School Time.

Halpern, R. (1999). After-school programs for low-income children: Promises and challenges. *Future of Children, 9*(3), 81–95.

Hargreaves, A. (1994). *Changing teachers, changing times: Teachers' work and culture in the postmodern age.* Toronto, Ontario, Canada: OISE Press.

Hofferth, S. L., & Jankuniene, Z. (2001). Life after school. *Educational Leadership, 58*(7), 19–23.

Jerald, C. D. (2001). *Dispelling the myth revisited: Preliminary findings from a nationwide analysis of "high-flying schools."* Washington, DC: Education Trust.

Klingner, J. (2004). The science of professional development. *Journal of Learning Disabilities, 37,* 248–255.

Kohler, A., & Lazarin, M. (2007). *Hispanic education in the United States: Statistical brief.* Washington, DC: National Council of La Raza.

Larsen, M., & Malen, B. (1997, March). *The elementary school principal's influence on teachers' curricular and instructional decisions.* Presentation at the annual meeting of the American Educational Research Association, Chicago, IL. (ERIC Document Reproduction Service No. ED409628)

Lave, J., & Wenger, E. (1991). *Situated learning: Legitimate peripheral participation.* Cambridge, England: Cambridge University Press.

Lee, O., & Fradd, S. (1998). Science for all, including students from non-English-language backgrounds. *Educational Researcher, 27*(4), 12–21.

Lovato, R. (2008, May 26). Juan Crow in Georgia. *The Nation, 286*(20), 20–24.

McDermott, P., Gormley, K., Rothenberg, J., & Hammer, J. (1995). The influence of classroom practica experiences on student teachers' thoughts about teaching. *Journal of Teacher Education, 46,* 184–191.

Mendel, C., Watson, R., & MacGregor, C. (2002). *A study of leadership behaviors of elementary principals compared with school climate.* Kansas City, MO: Southern Regional Council for Educational Administration.

Miles, M. B., & Huberman, M. A. (1994). *Qualitative data analysis: An expanded sourcebook* (2nd ed.). Thousand Oaks, CA: Sage.

National Center for Education Statistics. (2007). *The condition of education.* Washington, DC: U.S. Government Printing Office.

Noguera, P. (2003). *City schools and the American dream: Reclaiming the promise of public education.* New York, NY: Teachers College Press.

Orfield, G., & Eaton, S. (1996). *Dismantling desegregation: The quiet reversal of Brown v. Board of Education.* New York, NY: New Press.

Passel, J. S. (2006). *The size and characteristics of the unauthorized migrant population in the U.S.: Estimates based on the March 2005 Current Population Survey.* Washington, DC: Pew Hispanic Center.

Reich, R. B. (1992). *The work of nations: Preparing ourselves for 21st century capitalism.* New York, NY: First Vintage.

Rothstein, R. (1994). Immigration dilemmas: The debate over the changing face of America. In N. Mills (Ed.), *Arguing immigration* (pp. 48–66). New York, NY: Simon & Schuster.

Rothstein, R. (2002). *Out of balance: Our understanding of how schools affect society and how society affects schools.* Chicago, IL: Spencer Foundation.

Ruiz-de-Valasco, J., Fix, M., & Clewell, B. C. (2001). *Overlooked and underserved: Immigrant students in U.S. secondary schools.* Washington, DC: Urban Institute.

Shumow, L. (2001). *Academic effects of after-school programs.* Champaign, IL: ERIC Clearinghouse on Elementary and Early Childhood Education. (ERIC Document Reproduction Service No. ED458010)

Smith, J., & Malkin, M. (1997, November). Border region grows. *Migration News,* 10–20.

Suarez-Orozco, M., & Suarez-Orozco, C. (2008). *Learning a new land.* Cambridge, MA: Harvard University Press.

Takanishi, R. (2004). Leveling the playing field: Supporting immigrant children from birth to eight. *The Future of Children, 14*(2), 61–79.

U.S. Bureau of the Census. (2000). *Current population reports.* Washington, DC: Author.

Walpole, S., Justice, L. M., & Invernizzi, M. A. (2004). Closing the gap between research and practice: Case study of school-wide literacy reform. *Reading & Writing Quarterly: Overcoming Learning Difficulties, 20,* 261–283.

Weiss, C. H. (1998). *Evaluation: Methods for studying programs and policies* (2nd ed.). Upper Saddle River, NJ: Prentice Hall.

Wells, G. (1994). The complementary contributions of Halliday and Vygotsky to a "language-based theory of learning." *Linguistics and Education, 6,* 41–90.

Wenger, E. (1998). *Communities of practice: Learning, meaning, and identity.* Cambridge, England: Cambridge University Press.

Wenger, E. (2006). *Communities of practice: A brief introduction.* Retrieved from http://ewenger.com/theory/index.htm

Wilson, W. J. (1989). The underclass: Issues, perspectives, and public policy. *Annals of the American Academy of Political and Social Science, 501,* 182–192.

Wilson, W. (1997). *When work disappears: The world of the new urban poor.* New York, NY: Vintage.

Yin, R. (2002). *Case study research: Design and method.* Thousand Oaks, CA: Sage.

Urban School Reform, Family Support, and Student Achievement

KIERSTEN GREENE
JEAN ANYON

City University of New York, New York, New York, USA

Teachers and other education professionals find themselves in schools and districts bombarded by reforms—each one purporting to improve student achievement, particularly in reading and mathematics. This article lays the political economic groundwork of student achievement in urban areas in an attempt to contextualize the studies of literacy in this issue of Reading & Writing Quarterly: Overcoming Learning Difficulties. *As long as school reforms do not address the economic obstacles facing students from low-income families, significant, sustainable improvements in academic achievement in urban public schools and districts will remain beyond reach. However, financial and other social supports to low-income urban families can and do significantly increase the achievement of the children in those families. It is hoped that literacy reforms and other education reforms will take to heart the economic and social realities of schooling and act on them.*

It is widely known, and has long been of concern to U.S. policymakers, that the majority of students from low-income urban families score poorly on standardized tests (Lipman, 2004)—particularly in literacy. According to an analysis of the 2005 National Assessment of Educational Progress, 84% of low-income fourth-grade students in 11 of the nation's largest urban districts scored at or below the basic level in reading; 85% of low-income urban students at the eighth-grade level scored at or below the basic level in reading

(National Center for Education Statistics, 2007).[1] These percentages demonstrate that the current education system is not assisting the vast majority of students living in urban poverty to attain high, or even proficient, levels of achievement in reading. As one analysis stated, "We've rigged the system against the success of some of our most vulnerable children" (Education Trust, 2006, p. 1). Unfortunately, this is not a new story. Failing schools have been widely studied and are the protagonist in mainstream films such as *Freedom Writers* and popular books such as Dan Brown's (2007) *The Great Expectations School.* Failing urban systems are at the forefront of discussions among policymakers and education professionals and are the focus of school reforms such as the No Child Left Behind Act of 2001 (NCLB). Reforms that fill classrooms with increasing numbers of books and supplies, after-school tutoring programs, and calls for alternative pedagogical practices are both necessary and urgent, but they are not sufficient to raise the achievement of the majority of low-income students and schools. Without addressing the growing economic obstacles faced by students and families in low-income urban schools, goals such as the one in NCLB to have all students reading at grade level by 2014 are not feasible.

There is a vast literature on the relation between varying instructional approaches and student achievement in reading (Ross et al., 2004; Taylor, Pearson, Peterson, & Rodriguez, 2003; Teale & Gambrell, 2007). However, few of these researchers attend to the power of the economic system to determine educational opportunities. The authors are *not* arguing here that pedagogy and curriculum have no effect on student achievement. As Anyon (1980) demonstrated in an early study of schooling and social class, schooling can and often does mimic and mold the social class attitudes and abilities of students. What the authors *are* suggesting is that research on the achievement of low-income students must begin to more explicitly acknowledge the power of socioeconomic status (SES) to trump education policy and the efforts of teachers and administrators in urban schools and classrooms. With such acknowledgement, policy and practice that link education reform to *economic* reform can begin to deepen the difference educators make in the lives and futures of poor children. This article, then, situates literacy reform in the larger political economic context of school reform in urban districts.

---

[1]Kiersten Greene undertook this analysis and arrived at these figures by accessing the Analyze Data tool on the National Assessment of Educational Progress Data Explorer website (http://nces.ed.gov/nationsreportcard/naepdata/). "Low-income" refers to students eligible for free or reduced priced lunch. "Urban" students are those from the following school districts: Atlanta, Austin, Boston, Charlotte, Chicago, Cleveland, the District of Columbia, Houston, Los Angeles, New York City, and San Diego. National Assessment of Educational Progress scores are reported according to four levels: below basic, basic, proficient, and advanced.

Corroborating the tendency of social class to powerfully affect educational opportunity, "achievement gap" research has demonstrated that, although there are many reasons why some Black students in predominantly White suburban high schools score lower than suburban Whites on tests, the Black students whose scores are lower are often from families of lower SES than the district's Whites (Ferguson, 2002; see also Magnuson & Duncan, 2006).

SES affects school achievement in a number of ways; however, for the purposes of this article, it is the economic and social effects of poverty that are of the greatest concern. Although poverty may not directly prevent educational achievement, it can severely limit educational opportunities and access. Poverty forces individuals into exhausting situations, such as juggling multiple low-wage jobs and navigating seemingly endless, time-consuming systems of public welfare. In addition, research has shown that lower SES can detrimentally affect not only the general happiness of young children but also their cognitive development (Lee & Burkam, 2002). The frustrations and despair created by living in poverty in one of the richest countries in the world can certainly put a damper on the enthusiasm, effort, and expectations with which urban children and their families approach kindergarten–Grade 12 education—not only in reading, but in other content areas as well.

The next sections of this article place the issue of low-income urban families in the context of the fiscally stressed cities in which they live, describe the consequences of this poverty for urban children, and report research demonstrating that providing income and other social supports to poor families typically increases significantly the educational achievement of the children.

URBAN POVERTY, NEIGHBORHOODS, AND SCHOOLS

In order to understand the ways in which urban schools operate today, it is necessary to examine the historical events that produced the areas in which they are situated. For much of the 20th century, urban neighborhoods struggled to survive the devastating effects of widespread urban decay, and the schools were severely—and negatively—impacted by this decline (Anyon, 1997). Numerous federal policies—such as guidelines that prohibited banks from loaning money for the purposes of buying city properties or rehabilitating residences (also referred to as *redlining*)—led to crumbling inner cities. Housing stock plummeted, buildings decayed, and businesses sought investment elsewhere. As a further incentive to large businesses, the late 1940s and 1950s saw tax reductions offered to businesses that chose relocation (outside of the city) over renovation. And in the post–World War II period, developers and municipalities received federal (and state) subsidies and land grants to build highways, sewer and electric lines, homes and office buildings—in the suburbs, but not in the cities. Beginning in 1962, businesses were rewarded for establishing new industrial plants and equipment (as opposed to renovating ones that already existed), and large corporations were offered tax breaks. By the mid-1960s, many middle-class families had moved to the suburbs, and many remaining businesses—such as super-markets, banks, doctor's offices, department stores, hospitals, pharmacies, theaters, and movies—followed, leaving behind a trail of families living in poverty without enough resources to thrive.

The diminishing city tax base drastically affected education funding in most industrial cities as early as the 1930s. The city property tax base (which provided the major funding for education) continued to deteriorate following the Great Depression and remains low today. Indeed, many cities have extremely valuable downtown property (e.g., the financial centers in New York, Chicago, San Francisco, and Atlanta), but city, state, and federal corporate tax rates on this property are about the lowest on record. As a result, the wealthy corporations in these downtowns contribute little toward urban education and other city services (Anyon, 2005).

Contrary to the assumptions of education policy analysts who argue that "money doesn't matter," and contradicting federal legislation (e.g., NCLB) that assumes it does not, low urban property tax receipts and insuf-ficient additional school financing have devastating effects on public education. Schools are stripped of their access to funds for curriculum resources, advanced classes, small classes, repairs, and restorations when cities lose their property base. Unfortunately, the majority of city school systems have not seen enough recent increases in funding to counteract these economic setbacks despite decades of educational finance litigation to do so.

In 2001, the Education Trust, an independent, Washington, DC-based group that monitors and analyzes city districts' available funding, conducted a study that laid bare the stark realities of cities' continuous struggles with diminishing financial resources. *The Funding Gap: Low-Income and Minority Students Receive Fewer Dollars* reported that in the majority of states, school districts that educate the largest number of poor and minority students have fewer state and local dollars to spend—an average of $966 less per student—than districts with the least number of poor and minority students (Education Trust, 2001, p. 1; see also Education Trust, 2004).

When combined, these discrepancies in funding amount to significant gaps between schools. For example, in New York, the state with the largest funding difference, funding per student in high-poverty districts is $2,152 less than in low-poverty ones:

This gap translates into a difference of $860,800 between two elementary schools of 400 students each, enough to compete with elite suburban schools for the most qualified teachers and to provide the kinds of additional instructional time and other resources that research and data show can make a difference. (Education Trust, 2001, p. 2)

Per-student funding gaps translate into the following school-wide gaps per year in a typical elementary school of 400 students with classrooms of 25 students: in Illinois, $824,000; in Montana, $614,000; in Pennsylvania, $499,200; and in Michigan, $441,200 (p. 2).

From the decline of urban neighborhoods to the widening gap in school funding, schools that serve students from low-income families are being offered the short end of the stick more often than not. And no school reform effort—whether it calls for smaller class sizes, more books and classroom materials, after-school programs, higher standards, better teacher quality, or so on—can by itself reverse this trend.

URBAN CHILDREN AND THE EFFECTS OF SES ON ACHIEVEMENT

In 2001, almost 12 million children in America, or 16% of children, lived below the official federal poverty line; almost half of those (a little more than 5 million and including nearly a million African American children) lived in *extreme* poverty (less than half the poverty line, or $7,400 in annual income for a family of three). These disturbing figures represent an increase of 17% in the number of children living in extreme poverty from 2000, the end of the economic "boom" (Cauthen & Lu, 2001, p. 3; Dillon, 2003, p. 3; Lu, 2003, pp. 1–2).

Even more disturbing, however, is that when one applies the National Research Council criteria for poverty, defined by an annual income of up to 200% of the official poverty line, a full *38%* of children living in America, or 27 million students in the nation's schools, are identified as poor. Although official statistics do not designate them as such, these children live in poverty, and the hardships they face are almost as severe as those of children who are considered "officially" poor (Cauthen & Lu, 2001, p. 3; Lu, 2003, p. 1). By this revised measure, 57% of African American, 64% of Latino, and 34% of White children were poor in 2001 in the United States (Lu, 2003, p. 2). These sobering figures reveal a national scandal no longer central to discussions of American poverty, which generally assume that the majority of minority children are no longer poor. As these numbers demonstrate, however, the majority of Black and Latino children still suffer poverty.

Although federal policy may not define these low-income families as poor, some federal regulations certainly acknowledge that they are. The criterion used for reduced price or free lunch for schoolchildren, for example, includes almost 40% (39.9%) of U.S. students (and 69.8% of Black, 71.4% of Latino, and 22.7% of White students). The cutoff for reduced price lunch is 185% of the official poverty line and that for free lunch is 130% (National Center for Education Statistics, 2004, p. 114).

Social science research reveals the significant correlation between social class (or SES) and educational achievement; this research concludes that in general, the higher the resource background of a child's family, the higher the child's academic success (e.g., Lee & Burkam, 2002). For example, David Rusk, an independent scholar and demographer, studied the relationship between SES and educational achievement by identifying and analyzing percentages of low-income students in schools. He found that in communities across the United States, a full 65% to 85% of school variation in standardized test scores is explained by variations in the school's percentage of low-income students (Kahlenberg, 2003; National Center for Education Statistics, 2003; Rusk, 1999, p. 91).

The specific effects of growing up in poverty have also been documented, and it has been found that children's development—both in school and at home—is greatly affected by impoverished circumstances. For instance, poverty has been found to have consistently negative effects on children's cognitive growth; in addition, longitudinal studies demonstrate that family income consistently predicts children's academic and cognitive performance more than any other factor (Lee & Burkam, 2002). And persistent, extreme poverty has been shown to have more detrimental and long-lasting effects on children than temporary poverty, effects that increase as lack of access to resources and parental emotional stress mount. Finally, poor children tend to have more health and behavior difficulties than those from more affluent families, which mitigates against educational success (Bolger & Patterson, 1995; Duncan & Brooks-Gunn, 1997; Houser, Brown, & Prosser, 1998; McLoyd, 1998; McLoyd, Jayartne, Ceballo, & Borquez, 1994; Sugland, Zaslow, & Brooks-Gunn, 1995).

Valerie Lee and David Burkam (2002) demonstrated that there is indeed a direct correlation between student achievement and SES. Using data from the U.S. Department of Education, they analyzed differences in young children's achievement scores in literacy (and mathematics) by race, ethnicity, and SES as the children began kindergarten. The researchers also explored differences by social background in an array of children's home and family activities. The study found that by age 5, the average cognitive scores of children in the highest SES group were 60% greater than the scores of those in the lowest SES group. The cognitive deficits were significantly *less* closely related to race/ethnicity than social class: After race differences were taken into account, children from different SES groups achieved at different levels. In addition, the impact of family structure (e.g., being in a single-parent family) on cognitive skills and development was much smaller than the impact of either race or SES. Social class accounted for far more of the variation in academic achievement than any other factor.

Lee and Burkam (2002) also found that poor children enter kindergarten systematically lower quality elementary schools than their more affluent peers.

> However school quality is defined—in terms of higher student achievement, more school resources, more qualified teachers, more positive teacher attitudes, better neighborhood or school conditions, private vs. public schools—the least advantaged U.S. children begin their formal schooling in consistently lower-quality schools. This reinforces the inequalities that develop even before children reach school age. (p. 3; see also Entwistle & Alexander, 1997; Phillips, Crouse, & Ralph, 1998; Stipic & Ryan, 1997; White, 1982)

When examined together, studies of poverty, SES, cognitive development, and academic achievement suggest that programs to raise the incomes of poor families would greatly enhance both the cognitive development and life chances of children and improve children's opportunities for success in school and, later, in the economy.

INCREASED FAMILY SUPPORTS AND EDUCATIONAL ACHIEVEMENT

There is both explicit and implicit evidence that increased financial resources for families raise the educational achievement of poor children—in literacy as well as in other content areas. More research examining the correlation between family financial support and academic achievement must be conducted if experts hope to create long-term, sustained change for the better in urban schools.

A longitudinal study completed in 2003 found that improving family income reduced the negative (aggressive) social behavior of children and improved their school behavior and performance. The study was conducted over 8 years with a representative informant population of 1,420 children ages 9 to 13 in rural North Carolina, a quarter of whom were from a Cherokee reservation (Costello, Compton, Keeler, & Angold, 2003; O'Connor, 2003). When the study commenced, the majority of the child participants—68%— were living below the official poverty line. On average, the poorer children engaged more often in vandalism, stealing, bullying, stubbornness, and outbursts of anger than those who were not poor. However, halfway into the study, a local casino began distributing a percentage of its profits to tribal families in the area, the payments of which peaked at about $6,000 per person in the year 2001. During the latter 4 years of the study, when these funds were being distributed, psychiatric tests administered by the researchers showed that the negative behaviors of children in families who were no longer poor dropped to the same levels as among children whose families had never been poor (decreasing by 40%). Parents who moved out of poverty reported having more time to spend with their children, and the researchers identified better parenting behavior. The researchers also identified as important to both parents and children the psychological benefits of not being poor. Poverty puts stress on families, which can increase the likelihood of children developing behavioral problems. One parent in the study told researchers that

> the jobs [produced by the casino] give people the chance to pull themselves up by their bootstraps and get out of poverty. That carries over into less juvenile crime, less domestic violence, and an overall better living experience for families. (O'Connor, 2003, p. 2)

In March 2001, the Manpower Development Research Corporation published a synthesis of research on how welfare and work policies affect the children of single mothers (Morris, Huston, Duncan, Crosby, & Bos, 2001). Data gathered from evaluations of five programs that provided income supplements to poverty-wage workers (i.e., Florida's Family Transition Program, the Minnesota Family Investment Program, the National Evaluation of Welfare-to-Work Strategies, the New Hope program, and the Self-Sufficiency Project) were analyzed. The programs offered various supports to poverty-wage workers—income supplements, earnings disregards (i.e., rules that allow working welfare recipients to keep more of their income when they go to work), subsidized health care, employment services, counseling, supervised after-school activities for children and youth, and informal get-togethers with project staff. The analysis found that even relatively small income supplements to working parents (amounting to about $4,000 per year) improved children's elementary school achievement by about 10% to 15% of the average variation in the control groups (Morris et al., p. 20). Improvements were also seen on test scores and in ratings by parents and/or teachers. Although these effects may have been small, they were statistically significant and had "consistently positive impacts on children's [school] achievement" (p. 63). Long-term studies have also found that the achievement and behavior of young children can have important implications for their well-being in adolescence and adulthood (Caspi, Wright, Moffit, & Silva, 1998; Masten & Coatsworth, 1995). Moreover, even small differences in academic achievement at an early age can translate into significant differences later: "A program's effects on children, even if the effects are small, may continue to have implications over the course of their lives" (Entwistle & Alexander, 1997, p. 25).

The limited earning supplements provided by four of these programs were unable to bring their recipients above the poverty level; however, the significant improvements in the children's school achievement and behavior suggest that more substantial increases in family resources would more than likely improve both the educational and social futures of children living in poverty.

One program, New Hope, did provide an earning supplement that brought its recipients above poverty level. The children in these families showed particularly impressive improvements in behavior and educational achievement. The program ran from 1994 to 1998 in two inner city areas in Milwaukee, and candidates for the program had to live in one of two targeted areas, be 18 or older, be willing and able to work at least 30 hr per week, and have a household income at or below 150% of the federal poverty level (Huston et al., 2001). When they entered the study, nearly 90% of the adult participants were single or separated mothers with children, and 80% were receiving public assistance. Created by a nonprofit community-based organization, the program provided multiple benefits: the earnings supplement, subsidized health insurance, and subsidized child care. In addition, the program offered help with obtaining a job and provided a community service job (for up to 1 year) for those unable to find work elsewhere. Project staff also offered advice and support as needed. The annual cost of providing these benefits was $5,300 per family.

New Hope was evaluated at 2- and 5-year intervals using a random assignment research design. Following systematic outreach in the communities to identify eligible people, more than 1,300 low-income adults were enrolled to participate in the study. Half of the applicants were randomly assigned to a program group that received New Hope's benefits, whereas the other half were randomly assigned to a control group that was not eligible for the benefits. Both evaluations showed positive results (Bos, Huston, Duncan, Brock, & McLoyd, 1996; Huston et al., 2001). Although financial supplements in the New Hope program did indeed reduce the number of families in poverty, according to the study, both program and control groups reported similar levels of hardship, such as food insufficiency and financial insecurity. At the same time, the program positively impacted the parents' well-being and coping skills.

> Parents in the New Hope group were more aware of available sources of assistance and support in the community, such as where to find assistance with energy costs or housing problems. More of them also knew about the [Earned Income Tax Credit] and its support. A significant number of program families intentionally used the Earned Income Tax Credits as a savings plan for making major purchases, reducing debt, and stabilizing rent and other payments. Parents in New Hope also reported better physical health and fewer symptoms associated with depression than did parents in the control group. Ethnographic data revealed that many parents had children with disabilities or behavioral difficulties, and New Hope helped the parents achieve a difficult balance among work,

services, and parenting. The New Hope parents reported fewer problems controlling their children, and parents of adolescents reported more effective management (better control and less need for punishment). (Huston et al., p. 9)

The study also revealed how New Hope helped improve children's performance in school.

> At both the two-year and the five-year points, children in the program performed better than control group children on several measures of academic achievement, particularly on reading and literacy tests. After five years, they scored higher on a standardized test of reading skills, and their parents reported that they got higher grades in reading skills. (Huston et al., 2001, p. 13)

The effects were slightly more pronounced for boys than for girls. Compared with their control group counterparts, boys in New Hope received higher ratings of academic performance from their teachers and were more likely to expect to attend college at both the 2- and the 5-year assessments. "New Hope adolescents reported more engagement with schools, feelings of efficacy, and expectations to finish college than did their control group counterparts" (pp. 13–14).

Like New Hope, other programs have improved children's achievement by providing wage supplements and subsidized child care among other necessary family supports (Michaloupolos, Tattri, Miller, & Robins, 2002; Morris et al., 2001). The findings of the New Hope study coincide with the increased educational achievement of students identified in large-scale programs—"mobility programs"—whose main purpose is to offer assistance to families by helping them move from inner city neighborhoods to significantly more affluent and/or significantly less segregated metropolitan areas. The Gatraux program, the first of its kind, assisted in the relocation of families within the Chicago metropolitan area. The Hope VI program is a recent relocation effort funded by the federal government. Programs such as these are an integral part of redressing long-standing metropolitan-wide inequities in most U.S. cities.

It makes sense that school achievement improves as family resources increase: Parents with sufficient time and money are more able to nurture their children's development with private tutoring, lessons, sports and arts programs, and educationally useful visits to museums and concerts. These parents can transmit positive expectations of college acceptance and labor market preparation. And they will have, or be able to procure, the funds for these. Sociologist Annette Lareau (2003) dubbed this kind of childrearing the "concerted cultivation" by middle- and upper middle-class parents of the skills, talents, and futures of their children. Lareau found this kind of activity typical of the affluent African American as well as Caucasian families she studied. There is common sense in the attention of these parents to developing the capacities and cultural capital of their children: The social class resources purchased by affluence are certainly the educational "basics." They are demanded by curriculum and pedagogy and rewarded by colleges and the labor market.

IN CONCLUSION

It would make sense to increase the access of the urban poor to economic resources and support so that they too can afford the time, money, and energy to prepare their children for success in school. Depending on school reform to create the economic resources and capital that school success already requires is putting the cart before the horse. One cannot depend on public schools to create equitable opportunities for urban graduates in a society that denies the minority poor the economic resources to do so. Rather, society should provide—alongside equity-seeking educational reform—the financial base of support to urban families and communities that will lay the foundation for better resourced families and schools.

Thus, financial strength is the engine of systemic school reform. This article has presented evidence that increased access to family support has a positive effect on student achievement—not only in terms of literacy, but across the board. In order to continue to consider how to improve education—particularly for students from urban and low-income families—educational researchers and policymakers are urged to take into account the larger economic factors that influence school success. Schools are an integral part of neighborhoods and communities, and in order to improve schools that are failing, society must also improve the lives of the families whose children attend them. As long as policymakers continue to conceptualize education reform as disconnected from the larger structural systems and institutions that perpetuate poverty, segregation, and huge economic gaps between rich and poor, differences in academic achievement will remain an irresolvable quandary, and they will most likely never choose the tools that could build an educational system in which all children achieve to the best of their ability.

REFERENCES

Anyon, J. (1980). Social class and the hidden curriculum of work. *Journal of Education, 162*(1), 7–92.

Anyon, J. (1997). *Ghetto schooling: A political economy of urban educational reform.* New York, NY: Teachers College Press.

Anyon, J. (2005). *Radical possibilities: Public policy, urban education, and a new social movement.* New York, NY: Routledge.

Bolger, K., & Patterson, C. (1995). Psychosocial adjustment among children experiencing persistent and intermittent family economic hardship. *Child Development, 66,* 1107–1129.

Bos, J., Huston, A., Duncan, G., Brock, T., & McLoyd, V. (1996). *New hope for people with low incomes: Two-year results of a program to reduce poverty and reform welfare.* New York, NY: Manpower Development Research Corporation.

Brown, D. (2007). *The great expectations school.* New York, NY: Arcade.

Caspi, A., Wright, B., Moffit, E., & Silva, T. (1998). Early failure in the labor market: Childhood and adolescent predictors of unemployment in the transition to adulthood. *American Sociological Review, 63,* 424–451.

Cauthen, N., & Lu, H. (2001, August). *Living on the edge: Employment alone is not enough for America's low-income children and families* (Research Brief No. 1). New York, NY: Columbia University Press, Mailman School of Public Health.

Costello, J., Compton, S., Keeler, G., & Angold, A. (2003). Relationships between poverty and psychopathology: A natural experiment. *Journal of the American Medical Association, 290,* 2023–2029.

Dillon, S. (2003, April 30). Report finds number of black children in deep poverty rising. *New York Times.* Available from http://www.nytimes.com/2003/04/30/national/30POOR.html?scp=1&sq=report%20finds%20number%20of%20black%20children%20in%20deep%20poverty&st=cse

Duncan, G., & Brooks-Gunn, J. (Eds.). (1997). *Consequences of growing up poor.* New York, NY: Russell Sage Foundation.

Education Trust. (2001, March). *The funding gap: Low-income and minority students receive fewer dollars.* Washington, DC: Author.

Education Trust. (2004). *The funding gap 2004: Many states still shortchange low income and minority students.* Washington, DC: Author.

Education Trust. (2006). *Funding gaps 2006.* Washington, DC: Author.

Entwistle, D., & Alexander, K. (1997). *Children, schools, and inequality.* Boulder, CO: Westview Press.

Ferguson, R. F. (2002). *What doesn't meet the eye: Understanding and addressing racial disparities in high-achieving suburban high schools.* Retrieved from the North Central Regional Educational Laboratory website: http://www.ncrel.org/gap/ferg/

Houser, R., Brown, B., & Prosser, W. (1998). *Indicators of children's well-being.* New York, NY: Russell Sage Foundation.

Huston, A., Miller, C., Richburg-Hayes, L., Duncan, G., Eldred, C., Weisner, T., ... Redcross, C. (2001). *Summary report: New Hope for families and children: Five-year results of a program to reduce poverty and reform welfare.* New York, NY: Manpower Development Research Corporation.

Kahlenberg, R. (2003). *All together now: Creating middle-class schools through public school choice.* Washington, DC: Brookings Institution.

Lareau, A. (2003). *Unequal childhoods: Class, race, and family life.* Berkeley: University of California Press.

Lee, V., & Burkam, D. (2002). *Inequality at the starting gate: Social background and achievement at kindergarten entry.* Washington, DC: Educational Policy Institute.

Lipman, P. (2004). *High stakes testing: Inequality, globalization, and urban school reform*. New York, NY: RoutledgeFalmer.

Lu, H. (2003). *Low-income children in the United States*. New York, NY: Columbia University, Mailman School of Public Health.

Magnuson, K. A., & Duncan, G. J. (2006). The role of socioeconomic family resources in the black-white test score gap among young children. *Developmental Review, 26*, 365–399.

Masten, A., & Coatsworth, D. (1995). The structure and coherence of competence from childhood through adolescence. *Child Development, 66*, 1635–1659.

McLoyd, V. (1998). Children in poverty: Development, public policy, and practice. In W. Damon (Series Ed.), I. E. Sigel, & K. A. Renniger (Vol. Eds.), *Handbook of child psychology: Vol. 4. Child psychology in practice* (5th ed., pp. 135–208). New York, NY: Wiley.

McLoyd, V., Jayartne, T. E., Ceballo, R., & Borquez, J. (1994). Unemployment and work interruption among African-American single mothers: Effects on parenting and adolescent socio-emotional functioning. *Child Development, 65*, 562–589.

Michaloupolos, C., Tattri, D., Miller, C., & Robins, P. (2002). *Making work pay: Final report on the self-sufficiency project for long-term welfare recipients*. New York, NY: Manpower Development Research Corporation.

Morris, P., Huston, A., Duncan, G., Crosby, D., & Bos, J. (2001). *How welfare and work policies affect children: A synthesis of research*. Washington, DC: Manpower Development Research Corporation.

National Center for Education Statistics. (2003). *The condition of education: An annual snapshot, 2003*. Washington, DC: U.S. Department of Education.

National Center for Education Statistics. (2004). *The condition of education 2004* (NCES Report No. 2004-077). Washington, DC: U.S. Government Printing Office.

National Center for Education Statistics. (2007). [Raw data]. Retrieved July 18, 2007, from http://nces.ed.gov/nationsreportcard/naepdata/

O'Connor, A. (2003, October 21). Rise in income improves children's behavior. *New York Times*, 21–22.

Phillips, M., Crouse, J., & Ralph, J. (1998). Does the black/white test score gap widen after children enter school? In C. Jenks & M. Phillips (Eds.), *The black/white test score gap* (pp. 229–272). Washington, DC: Brookings Institution.

Ross, S., Nunnery, J., Goldfeder, E., McDonald, A., Rachor, R., Hornbeck, M., & Fleischman, S. (2004). Using school reform models to improve reading achievement: A longitudinal study of direct instruction and Success for All in an urban district. *Journal of Education for Students Placed at Risk, 9*, 357–388.

Rusk, D. (1999). *Inside game/outside game: Winning strategies for saving urban America*. Washington, DC: Brookings Institution.

Stipic, D., & Ryan, R. (1997). Economically disadvantaged preschoolers: Ready to learn but further to go. *Developmental Psychology, 33*, 711–723.

Sugland, B., Zaslow, M., & Brooks-Gunn, J. (1995). The early childhood HOME inventory and HOME short form in differing socio-cultural groups: Are there differences in underlying structure, internal consistency of subs cases, and patterns of prediction? *Journal of Family Issues, 16*, 632–663.

Taylor, B., Pearson, P., Peterson, D., & Rodriguez, M. (2003). Reading growth in high poverty classrooms: The influence of teacher practices that encourage cognitive engagement in literacy learning. *The Elementary School Journal*, *104*(1), 3–28.

Teale, W., & Gambrell, L. (2007). Raising urban students' literacy achievement by engaging in authentic, challenging work. *The Reading Teacher, 60*, 728–739.

White, K. (1982). The relationship between socioeconomic status and academic achievement. *Psychological Bulletin, 91*, 46–81.

The Short Supply of Saints: Limits on Replication of Models That "Beat the Odds"

TAMARA WILDER

University of Michigan, Ann Arbor, Michigan, USA

REBECCA JACOBSEN

Michigan State University, East Lansing, Michigan, USA

Researchers have identified effective practices that allow schools to "beat the odds" and close the reading achievement gap. Although identifying these practices is important, researchers have paid little attention to the work it takes to implement them. Through interviews with teachers who work at schools identified as beating the odds, this research documents the amount of work it takes to implement effective practices and demonstrates that this extraordinarily time-consuming work is difficult to sustain and not easily replicated. Therefore, experts must not rely on these practices alone to close the reading achievement gap.

The persistence of an achievement gap between low-income minority students and middle-class White students is a topic that has received a great deal of attention (Chubb & Loveless, 2002; Coleman et al., 1966; Jencks & Phillips, 1998; Lareau, 2000; Ogbu, 2003; Rothstein, 2004; Thernstrom & Thernstrom, 2003). In particular, the detrimental effect of poverty on reading achievement is well documented, with poverty being one of the largest correlates of reading achievement (Cunningham, 2006; Duncan & Seymour, 2000; Hart & Risley, 1995; Snow, Burns, & Griffin, 1998). Over the past 30 years, the reading achievement gap as measured by National Assessment of Educational Progress (NAEP) has narrowed only slightly. In 1975, the average gap in reading scores on the long-term NAEP assessment between Black and White 9-year-olds was 35 points; by 2004 that gap had shrunk to 26 points, a statistically significant albeit not enormous change given the effort expended on closing the gap. The Black–White reading achievement gap also persists for 13-year-olds, although it too has narrowed somewhat in the past 30 years: In 1975, the gap was 36 points, and by 2004 it had decreased to 22 points. The Hispanic–White gap has also narrowed over the past 30 years: For 9-year-olds the gap has narrowed from 34 points in 1975 to 21 points in 2004, and for 13-year-olds the gap has decreased from 30 to 24 points (Perie, Moran, & Lutkus, 2005). Although there has been progress in narrowing the reading gap over the past 30 years, that progress is inadequate. Black and Hispanic youth still score about three quarters of a standard deviation below White students on the NAEP reading assessments.

Although some educational researchers have begun to recognize and analyze the complexity of factors that contribute to these achievement gaps, the public and political leaders often see the problem in much simpler terms. They often conclude that the main cause of the achievement gap is failing public schools alone, and they ignore the impact of broader socio-economic factors on academic success (Rothstein, 2004). They conclude that if all schools had high-quality teachers who used a high-quality curriculum and effective teaching practices, all students, regardless of their socioeconomic status, would achieve at high levels and the reaching achievement gap would be eliminated. These conclusions are often based on narratives about schools that "beat the odds" (i.e., schools that enroll significant numbers of minority and low-income students and yet produce average or above-average test scores). Citing examples of schools that are beating the odds, some political leaders have argued that these schools demonstrate that dedicated teachers alone can close the achievement gap (see, e.g., Bush, 2003).

Schools that beat the odds often have been highlighted by researchers and the media for a reason: They are successful. A wide body of research exists on effective schools and effective literacy practices (Cunningham, 2006; Hoffman, 1991; Langer, 2001; Puma et al., 1997; Taylor, Pearson, Clark, & Walpole, 2000; Taylor, Pearson, Peterson, & Rodriguez, 2003; Taylor, Pressley, & Pearson, 2002). These researchers have specifically examined low-income and/or high-minority schools to identify how schools beat the odds. This research identifies the important practices of schools, programs, and teachers that lead to better than expected outcomes for student achievement.

But although the identification of such practices is important, little attention has been paid to the actual work it takes to implement these practices and whether simply asking other schools that do not beat the odds to adopt these practices is a realistic strategy for closing the reading achievement gap. After all, the schools that have beaten the odds may simply be extraordinary and their practices not easily replicated. Research that focuses exclusively on the practices of effective schools and teachers can too easily result in policies that are not replicable, because attention has not been paid to what it takes to implement such practices. Therefore, this article examines the actual work required to enact the practices that lead schools to beat the odds. This research asks the following questions: Are the teacher practices necessary to beat the odds sustainable and easily replicable? And can these practices be considered a viable solution for closing the reading achievement gap writ large?

Through interviews with teachers who work at a network of schools identified as beating the odds, the Knowledge Is Power Program (KIPP) Academy schools, this research demonstrates that the extraordinary work done by teachers to implement these practices is not so easily replicated. In fact, many of the teachers question their ability to keep up with the work. Although the teachers interviewed in this study offer insights into their best practices—practices that are similar to those identified by previous research—the wide-scale replication of these practices cannot be the only strategy for closing the reading achievement gap.

LITERATURE REVIEW

In order to beat the odds schools must have effective practices, effective teachers who are able to implement these practices, and the ability to hire and retain effective teachers. This review of the literature synthesizes many of the findings in these sometimes disparate areas of research and provides an understanding of what experts already know it takes to beat the odds.

Effective Schools

Consensus exists in the literature on the factors that allow schools serving disadvantaged populations to beat the odds. Factors that enable schools to be effective include shared goals among teachers, the principal, other school staff, and parents to improve student literacy achievement (Taylor et al., 2002); ongoing curricular improvement and maximum use of instructional time (Hoffman, 1991); strong building leadership (Hoffman, 1991; Puma et al., 1997; Taylor et al., 2002); strong staff communication and collaboration (Cunningham, 2006; Taylor et al., 2000, 2002); ongoing professional development (Cunningham, 2006; Taylor et al., 2002); systematic utilization of student assessment data (Cunningham, 2006; Taylor et al., 2000, 2002); strong, positive home–school relationships (Hoffman, 1991; Taylor et al., 2000, 2002); a clear school mission (Hoffman, 1991); high expectations (Hoffman, 1991); safe, orderly school environments (Hoffman, 1991; Puma et al., 1997); and lower than average student and teacher mobility (Puma et al., 1997).

Another critical factor for effective high-poverty schools is the importance of learning, growth, and change over an extended period of time.

In their study of the impact of the Center for the Improvement of Early Reading Achievement School Change Framework in 13 schools across the United States, Taylor, Pearson, Peterson, and Rodriguez (2005) found that the more elements of the framework a school implemented, the greater the growth in students' reading comprehension and fluency. After the 1-year evaluation, the effect was significant but small. Yet when examined over a 2-year period, the effect had grown to be moderately large. Taylor et al. (2005) concluded that the increase in effect over time "highlights the importance of sustained school improvement efforts" (p. 64).

Much of the literature suggests that in addition to sustained reform, teacher and principal collaboration is an essential characteristic of effective high-poverty schools. Collaboration among teachers and the principal in a school is an important aspect in the realization of many of the characteristics of an effective school. Teachers and principals must collaborate to ensure that there is agreement on the goal of improved student literacy and consensus around the school's curricula, practices, and expectations that will enable it to realize that shared goal. Teachers must collaborate to determine how best to meet students' needs. Professional development activities in which teachers learn together are recommended, as are practices in which teachers evaluate student assessment together. In her examination of six successful high-poverty schools, Cunningham (2006) found that time put aside to meet as a faculty was essential to the success of each school. Teacher collaboration is crucial to effective schools.

Effective Teachers

Through collaboration, teachers generate a shared sense of commitment to their school's goals and practices, which is an important feature of successful schools (Taylor et al., 2005). Furthermore, high levels of teacher initiative and perseverance differentiate teachers in successful schools from those in other schools (Taylor et al., 2005). Schools that beat the odds in reading have teachers who buy in to their literacy reform plans; teacher support for change is crucial (Taylor et al., 2005).

In addition to collaboration, teachers must engage in effective practices in order to beat the odds in reading. The literature suggests that one such practice is the use of data-driven decision making (Taylor et al., 2005). The use of frequent reading assessments of students with results tied back to instruction is a practice found in effective classrooms.

Effective teachers are an essential piece of successful schools. Taylor, Pearson, Peterson, and Rodriguez (2003) investigated how teaching practices affected students' reading achievement in nine high-poverty schools. They selected 88 teachers and 9 randomly assigned students per classroom to engage in a literacy reform program. They found that the teaching practice variables explained substantial variation in student growth on multiple measures of reading achievement. More specifically, teachers who emphasized higher order thinking skills induced greater growth in reading among targeted students.

Not only does the practice of emphasizing higher order thinking skills lead to positive reading gains, but engaging in high-level questioning, coaching students in strategies to apply their word recognition skills to everyday reading, and giving students more time for independent reading are all teacher practices found in effective classrooms (Taylor et al., 2000). Small-group reading instruction has also been found to be an effective practice (Taylor et al., 2000).

Hiring and Retaining Effective Teachers

Researchers have found that teacher effectiveness is a major school factor influencing student academic gains (Rice, 2003; Sanders & Horn, 1998; Wright, Horn, & Sanders, 1997). In short, teachers matter. But finding and keeping highly qualified teachers is not easy for any school and may be an especially acute problem for high-poverty and/or high-minority schools. Predictions of teacher shortages have been reported for the past two decades (Gardner, 1983; Johnson et al., 2001; National Commission on Teaching, 1997). Early reports often cited a rising demand for teachers due to increasing student enrollments and increasing teacher retirements as the cause for the looming shortage. More recent research, however, has instead turned to teacher turnover as the real issue to be addressed (Ingersoll, 2001, 2003; Tye & O'Brien, 2002). Indeed, Ingersoll (2001) noted in his work that turnover among teachers appears to be higher than in many other occupations, and even compared to a similar profession, such as nursing, the turnover rate is approximately 3 percentage points higher. Because of the large number of teachers needed to staff all schools, the constant churning of the teacher workforce poses many challenges to the stability of schools, as new teachers must become familiar with a school's routines, policies, and practices. Moreover, the turnover rates are even higher in high-poverty and urban schools (Darling-Hammond, 2003; Guarino, Santibanez, & Daley, 2006; Ingersoll, 2001). Large rates of instability in a school's staff can hurt student achievement. Darling-Hammond noted that "churning in the beginning teaching force reduces productivity in education" (p. 8), as the system never reaps the benefits from the development of these young teachers into seasoned professionals.

The causes behind such turnover are often linked to organizational problems within schools. Several studies have reported teachers' reasons for leaving the classroom and have identified key issues that are repeatedly mentioned across nearly all of the studies in this area. One of the most often cited reasons for leaving teaching is low salaries. In his study of the Teacher

Follow Up Survey, Ingersoll (2003) found that the strategy most recommended by teachers to aid in retention was to increase salaries.

But salaries alone will not solve the turnover problem. Teachers also cite a number of organizational problems in school that lead to job dissatisfaction. Teachers often mention the lack of student discipline and motivation as a major source of frustration in their work. In the third Phi Delta Kappa poll of teachers' attitudes toward the public schools, teachers rated student discipline as one of the biggest concerns schools face (Langdon, 1996). In their longitudinal study of a cohort of new teachers, Johnson and Birkeland (2002) found that the voluntary movers, or those who chose to switch schools or districts, often described their schools as places where "disrespect and disruption were taken for granted as inevitable" (p. 27).

Although teachers express frustration with the lack of student discipline, they do not always lay blame with the students alone. Rather, teachers often cite the lack of administrative support or lack of supportive colleagues to help them deal with disruptive students. Some of the "leavers" in the Johnson and Birkeland (2002) study described administrators who were "ineffective or intimidating" and discussed "the disappointment of colleagues who failed to support them as they struggled to teach" (p. 21). Such support is critical for new teachers and yet it was so often cited as lacking. In a different study that looked at factors teachers cited as keeping them in the profession, Certo and Fox (2002) found that collegial relationships were important. Specifically, teachers noted that it was important that their schools had provided teachers with time to collaborate and build these supportive networks. Malloy and Wohlstetter (2003) found that like-minded and hard-working colleagues were a commonly discussed draw for teachers to work in charter schools. The teachers they interviewed enjoyed working with colleagues who were "experts" and "determined, dedicated teachers" (p. 234). In general, studies that have examined the Schools and Staffing Survey have found that teachers who reported being in schools where there was a higher degree of collegial support reported lower rates of turnover (Guarino et al., 2006).

All of these factors—low pay, lack of administrative support, disruptive student behavior, and lack of collegial support—are important in explaining why retaining effective teachers remains a challenge for high-poverty/high-minority schools. There is reason to believe that schools that beat the odds may have created positive environments for teachers by developing many of the practices found to be effective for maintaining a stable teaching staff: allowing more time for collaboration and teamwork, attracting dedicated and like-minded teachers, and offering increased pay and a disciplined and supportive work atmosphere. It is possible that such a structure has positive effects not only on students but also on staff, which helps these schools beat the odds.

METHODS

Case Selection: Schools That Beat the Odds—The KIPP Academy Network

To understand the sustainability and replicability of the work of teachers in schools that beat the odds, one must select schools. Several schools have been highlighted by researchers and the media as beating the odds. One group of schools in particular that has received a good deal of attention in the media for its success in improving the academic achievement of disadvantaged children is the KIPP Academy, a network of charter schools. KIPP Academy schools and their teachers provide an excellent case study of what it takes to beat the odds.

The KIPP model encompasses many of the characteristics of effective schools. The essence of the KIPP model is well captured in the following statement from the KIPP website: "By providing a safe and structured learning environment, more time in school, and high-quality teachers, KIPP schools have helped students make significant academic gains" (KIPP, n.d.-c). The KIPP model is structured such that each school is run by its own school leader, who is recruited and trained by the KIPP Foundation and governed by a local board of directors. KIPP schools are free to choose their own curricula and instructional strategies. What ties all KIPP schools together is the implementation of the Five Pillars and demonstrable positive student achievement gains. The Five Pillars seem to come directly from the literature on effective high-poverty schools. The Five Pillars are High Expectations, Choice and Commitment, More Time, Power to Lead, and Focus on Results (see the Appendix for a description of each pillar).

Reports of KIPP's success have appeared in *USA Today*, *The New York Times*, and *The Washington Post*, and the schools have been featured in television programs such as PBS's *Making Schools Work* with Hedrick Smith and *60 Minutes*. In addition, several books and research reports have argued that although KIPP schools enroll students who are typical of urban, regular public schools, the students' scores are typically higher after just a few years than scores for Black and Hispanic urban children generally in regular public schools (Education Trust, 2003; Fuller, 2001; Thernstrom & Thernstrom, 2003). Some have argued that KIPP's success is due to the fact that KIPP schools make no excuses based on the students' backgrounds, and instead students and teachers simply work harder to achieve more (Education Trust, 2003; Fuller, 2001; Thernstrom & Thernstrom, 2003).

Test score data also support the assertion that KIPP schools beat the odds. The majority of KIPP schools produce positive gains in student achievement as measured by average percentile rankings on the Stanford

Achievement Test. For example, gains in reading are found from the beginning of fifth grade to the end of fifth grade in all but one of the schools for which there are data. The first-year gains are greater than 10 percentage points in 27 of the 37 schools for which there are data, and in 9 schools the gains are greater than 25 percentage points. Among students tracked over time from fifth to eighth grade, as has been done in seven of the KIPP middle schools, yearly gains on the reading Stanford Achievement Test have also been documented. Typically, the gains range from 7 to 36 points, which are quite large gains over 4 years (KIPP, 2006). In addition, long-term positive academic outcomes have also been documented, with almost 80% of students who complete eighth grade at a KIPP school matriculating to college (KIPP, n.d.-a). However, the large reading gains found in KIPP schools are particularly notable because reading achievement is more difficult for schools to influence because of the strong link between the home environment and reading ability (Rothstein, 2004).

More sophisticated analyses of student achievement in KIPP schools have documented the significant growth in literacy found among KIPP students. In a study of three recently opened KIPP schools, Doran and Drury (2002) used Normal Curve Equivalent scores on the Stanford 9, state test scores, and prior test score data in longitudinal multivariate statistical models to demonstrate that, regardless of student background or label, the schools increased their students' academic achievement levels. A study of the Memphis KIPP DIAMOND Academy used a quasi-experimental design that matched KIPP students to similar students from neighborhood schools. This study found that the KIPP school had positive, statistically significant effects on student achievement (Gallagher & Ross, 2005). In a larger study that included 1,800 fifth-grade students at 24 KIPP schools, a pre- and posttest design found positive, statistically significant gains on the Stanford 9 and 10 for cohorts in all but two of the schools (Education Policy Institute, 2005).

Two additional studies have found KIPP schools to positively affect student achievement but noted a challenge in these schools: staff turnover. An investigation of a KIPP school in Colorado concluded that the biggest challenge the school faced in its first year was staff turnover (Anderson & DeCesare, 2006). Furthermore, a study of San Francisco area KIPP schools found that 3 out of 4 of the teachers described "feeling overwhelmed by the demands of the job and expressed concern about how long they can per-sist in the job if the demands remain the same" (David et al., 2006, p. 28). Regarding the sustainability of the KIPP model, some of the teachers made statements such as "This job eats people alive" and "I don't think the KIPP model is designed for keeping teachers around," and a principal said, "Well, you put in two good years and KIPP is like dog years. It's not a school that will encourage me to stay for five years" (pp. 28–29).

However, KIPP's sustained success in raising the academic achievement of low-income and minority students over the past 12 years has led to an expansion of the KIPP network. In the 2007–2008 school year the KIPP network increased its number of schools by almost 20%, adding nine new schools. KIPP is also planning major growth in Houston, Texas, that will result in 35 new KIPP schools. But is major expansion of the KIPP model in Houston and around the country possible? How replicable are models that beat the odds, and, thus, can they be considered a viable solution for closing the reading achievement gap writ large?

KIPP's popularity, the widespread agreement about its success, along with the reading test score data make it an excellent case study of what it takes for teachers to implement the best practices identified in previous research. KIPP teachers can provide insight into whether sustaining and replicating such work is possible.

Teacher Selection: Interviewing Teachers Who Work to Beat the Odds at KIPP Schools

To better understand the demands of implementing the necessary practices to beat the odds and whether these practices are sustainable and easily replicated from a teacher's perspective, this study conducted telephone interviews with a sample of KIPP teachers from around the nation. Respondents were recruited via e-mails sent to all KIPP teachers with publicly available e-mail addresses. Of the 48 KIPP charter schools in operation at the time of recruitment, e-mails were sent to all teachers at 38 of the schools. A first wave of e-mails was sent in the late spring of 2007, and a second wave of follow-up e-mails was sent in the late summer of 2007. After receiving a recruitment e-mail explaining the purpose of the study and the time commitment associated with participating, interested teachers contacted the authors to set up interviews.

This method of recruitment does introduce possible self-selection bias that may threaten the validity of this study. The self-selection of teachers into the sample may have resulted in a biased sample. Teachers who volunteer to participate in a survey regarding their effective practices may be the most frustrated with these practices. However, those who opted to participate in the study might be the most satisfied and eager to share their success. Although patterns did emerge from the interviews, the participants expressed a range of views suggesting that despite self-selection, the sample was likely to be representative. Therefore, the authors are confident that the results presented are valid praises and critiques.

A total of 24 teachers responded to the recruitment e-mail, but scheduling conflicts and the lack of organizational approval[1] decreased the size of the

---

[1]The authors did not pursue approval or assistance from the KIPP Foundation, as respondent confidentiality was of the utmost importance and endorsement from the respondents' employer was seen as a threat to validity.

final sample to 12 teachers. In the end, semistructured telephone interviews were completed by the authors. Each teacher was interviewed once, and the interview lasted approximately 30 min. These interviews served as the main source of data; however, additional documents from KIPP schools regarding the school structure and mission were also reviewed. Although the sample size was small, the consistency among respondents' answers and the geographically and demographically diverse sample gave the authors confidence about the accuracy and possible generalizability of the responses.

All major geographic regions of the United States were represented in the sample: Teachers were interviewed in nine cities in five states throughout the Northeast, Midwest, West, and South and in the District of Columbia. The respondents were between the ages of 25 and 55 years old. The gender breakdown of the sample was evenly split between men and women. Four of the respondents had children. Ten of the respondents were White. Each of the schools the respondents came from had been in operation for at least 4 years. The experience level of the teachers ranged from a minimum of 3 years to more than 10 years.

During the interviews, the respondents were asked to describe time allocations during a typical week, to discuss the types of activities or practices they engaged in to ensure student success, and to discuss their prior teaching experiences and their career expectations. In addition, respondents were asked to estimate the average amount of time devoted to implementing their successful practices. By asking the questions using multiple formats, the authors obtained more accurate results.

Based on the research questions, an initial set of descriptive codes was developed (Miles & Huberman, 1984). The data were coded for five themes: enjoyable aspects of the job, changes one hoped to see in the current job, plans to stay at or leave one's current school, successful practices to ensure student success, and future career aspirations. Each author used these codes to find relevant sections in each interview that were then organized in a database for further analysis. Differences between the authors' coding of each interview were resolved, and a master database was developed. This database allowed the authors to look across interviews for further analysis.

Because the teachers offered a range of responses within each of the five major themes, a second set of interpretive codes was developed to understand the implications of the teachers' responses for the sustainability of schools that beat the odds. Statements in each of the five themes were analyzed and coded according to emergent patterns. Enjoyable aspects of the job were coded as students, teachers, school environment, and professional autonomy. Statements pertaining to changes one hoped to see in the current job were coded as student discipline, student expectations, grade level taught, and reduced hours. Statements regarding plans to leave or stay at the current job were coded as positive, negative, questionable, or neutral. Successful practices were coded as system use of student data, frequent assessments, active engagement of students in lessons, differential instruction, and collaboration among teachers. Future career aspirations were coded as remaining in teaching, educational administration, or leaving the field of education. These interpretive codes allowed the authors to draw conclusions about teachers' general beliefs and attitudes within each of the five themes.

In addition, the reported average number of hours required to implement the teachers' successful practices was analyzed. This was a two-part process. First, respondents were asked to estimate the amount of time spent in school, the amount of time spent working outside of school, and the amount of time spent working on the weekends. These time allocations were added by the authors to obtain a weekly total. Second, because retrospective reporting can be inaccurate and time estimations can be prone to over- or underreporting (Converse & Presser, 1986), the total time spent working in a day was calculated from the respondents' "walk throughs" of their typical days. Respondents were asked to outline their daily activities hour by hour.[2] This resulted in an average number of hours worked daily, which was used to verify the hours reported in the previous question. In only three cases the estimates obtained through these two different methods differed by more than 5 hr. In these cases, the average of the two estimates is reported.

RESULTS

Four themes emerged from the KIPP teachers. The results are organized here by the following themes: practices that help students succeed, the required time commitment, teacher retention, and the long-term sustainability of this time commitment. Sustainability of the time commitment was the theme most often discussed, and therefore it receives the most attention here.

Most Important Practice to Beat the Odds

Many of the teachers reported that their most important practice was one that had already been identified by research on effective schools and effective teachers. In particular, KIPP teachers identified the following important practices as critical to their success: using student data systematically; working collectively as a staff to create a safe, orderly environment; and developing lessons that are engaging and challenging for students.

---

[2]This hour-by-hour breakdown often resulted in respondents revising their previous claims of the number of hours worked per week. Most often, the number of hours increased as respondents actually took count of their typical daily activities.

Many of the KIPP teachers noted that they used data to inform their instructional choices. Colleen[3] in particular noted how she made extensive use of data to ensure that all of her students were achieving:

> I give quizzes twice a week and a test every other week. That assessment really drives my instruction. The kids and I both keep track of their skills mastery...and that really gives a sense of purpose to everything that we do in class.

Sarah also noted that "really using data to plan" was the most important practice that she engaged in to ensure her students' success. Jeff said that the first thing a teacher needs to know is "what your goals are as a teacher. You really need to know where you are trying to get your students." Using diagnostic testing to make sure that his students were hitting these goals was critical, according to Jeff. Consistent with previous research, the teachers felt that the systematic use of data was a critical practice to helping schools beat the odds (Taylor et al., 2000, 2002).

Several teachers also noted that a key to success was the collective development of a safe and orderly learning environment. Dan even noted that his school had developed a 62-page document detailing all of the components that went into developing the many systems and shared culture of the school. He said that it covered everything from "when you sharpen your pencil" to "how to listen to a discussion." Furthermore, Dan noted that the shared development of a positive school culture did not exist in his previous school and that he had been "trying to do it on my own." He felt that "trying to do it alone" hindered the success of his students. He felt that the shared culture of the KIPP school was the "number one thing that works" because it "provides a really safe and exciting place for the kids to learn." Similarly, Patty noted that the shared school culture was very important and allowed everyone to "be very focused on student achievement." Even Keith, who described the school structures as "rigid," stated that it was the most important practice that led to student success.

Finally, the teachers also discussed the work that went into developing their lessons as being a critical component to their success. Eight of the teachers interviewed specifically said that they worked to develop lessons that were "engaging" for students. The teachers often coupled engagement with the development of critical thinking. For example, Jeff stated that making sure his lessons were engaging was a key practice to his success but then elaborated that engagement meant that the students were being "challenged intellectually." He said that he wanted to create lessons that were "fun and exciting" but that also got students "to think

---

[3]All names are pseudonyms.

and process the information." Similarly, Lucy said that learning to facilitate discussions that are really engaging was a key practice she worked to incorporate into her teaching. Abby worked to get her students "to invest in the [learning] process," and she thought that this sort of engagement was important to student success. The teachers felt that by engaging students they were able to push student learning by incorporating more challenging and thoughtful activities.

The teachers interviewed in this study echoed many of the effective practices that have been identified by previous research. KIPP teachers used practices known to be effective at raising student achievement, and these practices were important to their school's ability to beat the odds. However, in terms of implementing these best practices, the teachers also explained the serious time commitment it took to systematically use data to drive instruction, to collaborate in developing a structured and effective learning environment, and to develop engaging and challenging lessons. The time required to effectively implement these practices was significant, as is shown in the next section.

Time Commitment

One of the five pillars essential to the success of the KIPP model is More Time, and this pillar is certainly fulfilled (see the Appendix for a full description of the five pillars). The teachers interviewed reported that they typically spent between 10 and 14 hr a day at their schools. Most of the teachers also reported that they spent additional time working during the evenings and on weekends. In the evenings, teachers may grade assignments, prepare for the next day, help students over the phone, or talk with parents. Most teachers reported working for approximately 1 to 2 hr on such activities each night.

Student phone calls, a unique aspect of the KIPP model, sometimes took up the majority of the evening work time. Many teachers reported frequently receiving phone calls in the evening hours. KIPP students are encouraged, as part of the "no excuses" philosophy, to call teachers in the evenings with questions and issues pertaining to their homework assignments. The teachers claimed that students take advantage of this after-hours resource but differentially (in terms of timing, grade level, subject taught, and type of student) throughout the year. Colleen reported that at the beginning of the year, particularly in the fifth grade (often the beginning of students' KIPP experience), students are far more likely to call the teacher with questions. Most of the teachers found this unique practice important for the development of strong academic and social skills in the students. Jack stated, "It's really cool to see kids take on the responsibility of calling grown-ups and having grown-up conversations. I think that is an invaluable tool for kids. They leave very professional messages." Reiterating the process through which the "phone call" policy builds students' social skills, Colleen described the following outcome: "The other thing that happens is that as the year progresses, they feel more confident calling each other opposed to calling me and so that is fantastic."

Although the teachers maintained that this practice is extremely beneficial to students, requiring teachers to be "on call" every day after regular school hours elongates the teachers' work hours well into the evening. Being on call after working 10- to 14-hr days can be exhausting for some of the teachers. When discussing this policy, Jack noted, "You feel like you are always on the hook." Consequently, Jack alluded to an unspoken classroom policy that students are not to call after 9 p.m. and that if they do, they will get voicemail. While searching for a new teaching position, Jared made a point of asking prospective schools about their on-call policy. Jared stated, "I asked if they give their teachers cell phones and expect their teachers to be on call 24 hours a day, which is a habit that I know is important, but is also very invasive."

Teachers also discussed working a half day on at least one Saturday a month. All together, the KIPP teachers reported working between 55 and 80 hr each week. Seven of the teachers reported that their average hours worked per week fell between 60 and 70 hr. Of the remaining teachers, three said they worked more than 70 hr and two said they worked less than 60 hr.[4] These findings suggest that, on average, KIPP teachers work more hours per day than other teachers. According to the teachers, the increased hours were a significant factor necessary to achieve a high degree of student success. When asked what makes their KIPP school successful, Dan stated, "There is really no magic about KIPP. It is really just a lot of hard work."

Teacher Retention: What Keeps KIPP Teachers?

Despite the substantial time commitment KIPP teachers make during and after school, many teachers expressed satisfaction working for a KIPP school. Specifically, the teachers were asked to reflect on the one aspect that they enjoyed most about the job. Many teachers, 8 of the 12, mentioned that it was the dedicated and professional faculty that they enjoyed most. Specifically, the teachers responded with "the cooperative relationship between staff, cohesive group," "respect and trust among staff and principal," and "the intellectual atmosphere, great teachers." It was not uncommon for the

---

[4]Although self-reports may overestimate or underestimate the actual time, several questions in various formats were asked to verify the responses. When answers to different questions varied, averages were used.

teachers to refer to their colleagues as "brilliant," "gifted," and "inspiring." Abby summarized it by saying the following:

> The nice thing about the KIPP model is that everybody is on the same page. Everybody is working hard to impact lives and we support each other. There is no weak link because people are fired. We are all marching together.

Patty commented that being around similarly hard-working staff members was different from previous school experiences:

> I have always been the teacher that comes early, leaves late, and does the extra things like offering tutoring, paying out of pocket, or running extra curricular activities. The nice thing about being at a KIPP school is that every teacher does that. I am with people that have the same mindset. That is what keeps me going.

The importance of the like-minded staff led several of the teachers to say that they would not leave a KIPP school unless they were able to find a similarly like-minded set of staff. These comments point out that such dedication is important not only to the success of the students but also to keeping KIPP teachers inspired, motivated, and committed.

Teachers also frequently commented that the best thing about the KIPP schools was the students. Not surprisingly, the teachers repeatedly expressed a great deal of enjoyment in watching their students succeed and grow. Phrases like "I love the children," "I enjoy seeing them grow and excel," and "The students are amazing" were often used to describe the best thing about working at a KIPP school. Dan stated, "I would say the quality of work that our students are producing is equally important [as the talented and inspiring staff]. The students put together amazing work every day and I am really excited to see them each day." The combination of dedicated staff working with dedicated students was important for nearly all of the teachers interviewed. The school culture of hard work and dedication for both teachers and students encouraged teacher retention. Teachers believed that this shared commitment was a necessary component to their desire to stay at a KIPP school. But many of the teachers interviewed also questioned whether they would be able to continue the pace of the job, as is discussed in the next section.

Sustainability of Time Commitment

Does the increased time commitment impact teachers' retention at KIPP schools? This question is critical to understanding the sustainability and replicability of the KIPP model, but this issue has yet to be addressed in the school reform and teacher retention literatures.

Although the teachers described a positive environment in which to work, and although the literature suggests that this is key to retaining teachers, many teachers reported uncertainty about their ability to remain dedicated KIPP teachers. Furthermore, teachers worried about the availability of committed individuals willing to make the sacrifices in terms of time and personal life necessary for succeeding at a KIPP school. Echoing this concern, Dan stated,

> It is going to be hard to find a system-wide or a country-wide workforce of dedicated and brilliant individuals that could take their wares elsewhere and get paid a lot more money and could do the same job for an extended period of time. That could be very challenging to replicate.

Furthermore, Aaron noted,

> The biggest detriment to the KIPP schooling system is the high turnover rate for teachers. It is the biggest detriment to replicating the KIPP school model on a larger scale. I just happen to be one of the odd freaks out in the world that has my life in the classroom. I don't think there really are a lot of people that do that.

Abby considered becoming a KIPP school leader and opening a new KIPP school. However, the lack of enough dedicated teachers was a "huge roadblock" that eventually deterred Abby from pursuing this path. Abby explained that as a member of the school's hiring committee she saw that the school would interview sometimes up to 30 teachers and not find a single teacher that they felt was qualified. Therefore, Abby noted,

> There are not enough teachers. There are high expectations for the teachers, not just the students, and it's a huge problem. We have been talking about how to find new teachers but where do we go [to find them]? It is a big problem.

Not all teachers felt so strongly that the model was unsustainable. For example, Jeff remarked,

> I think it is sustainable for the right type of person . . . it has to be something that you really believe in and it has to be something that you really love. I wouldn't be able to do it if my spouse didn't support me. I wouldn't be able to do it if we both didn't work really hard to ensure that we spend time together as a family. So I do think it is sustainable . . . I just think that there are probably less people that would do it.

Finding a healthy balance between being a KIPP teacher and having a life outside of school, or even between being a KIPP teacher and being physically healthy, was difficult for many of the teachers interviewed. Time and again, teachers referred to this challenge, and it often impacted their views about future career plans. For example, Dan noted, "The hardest thing is the life–work balance. It is a demanding job, especially with a couple of kids and a family. To balance your time as a teacher is hard."

Although recognizing the successful practice of providing students with more time, Jack and Patty both questioned the impact that this additional time had on their personal lives. Jack stated,

> I think that the time is beneficial to kids in some ways, in many ways. But I really think that as teachers we're trying to develop and socialize the families, and some of us are getting married and it doesn't allow much time for you to develop yourself as a person other than as a teacher.

Similarly, Patty too noted the dilemma between work and personal life:

> I would like to stay, but I don't know how much longer I can put in 60- or 70-hour work weeks because it leaves very little time for dating or a social life. I constantly find myself sacrificing my own personal goals and life choices for the sake of my students.

Like Patty, Sarah questioned whether this successful practice would be possible in her future. She stated, "The time thing is definitely a huge issue. Right now I am childless, but I do wonder about it when I start a family."

More than any of the other teachers interviewed, Jared's personal sense of struggle with the additional time needed to beat the odds came through in his interview:

> I think over time [the difficulty in taking sick time because of a lack of substitutes and a sick day system] is a reason why I don't think that I can stay with KIPP long term. I love my time here. There's a lot that I love about the school, but sustainability wise, I don't think that it is realistic for people to work from 6:45 a.m. to 5:30 p.m. at the very least and to feel guilty to go to the doctor or take care of a personal matter. I am lucky I don't have a family. I'm not married. For the most part, I see a lot of people at my school who work overtime, work very long hours, and take a lot out of themselves and maybe they don't have families, maybe they aren't taking care of themselves physically. I don't see a lot of people here who have children, who have families, who have lives outside of school that are exactly what they want. When I look at that I just think, you know in the next couple of years, I would like to move towards getting married and having a family . . . From tutoring, from taking phone calls at home to just the work of being a teacher and trying to do your best every day, you just get worn down and you just start searching for what are other ways you can do the same kinds of things we do here but not have it take the gigantic physical toll.

Once again, these views are not shocking. Working 10 to 14 hr in school each day plus evenings and during some weekends surely makes it difficult to maintain a healthy social and personal life. There was some variation between the KIPP schools, as some principals had begun to respond to the issues of starting a family. Dan reported that schedule changes allowed "less face time" at the school. But few teachers saw systematic changes being implemented that would decrease the numbers of hours required to achieve the same levels of student success.

The time commitment required of KIPP teachers can often lead to burnout and turnover. For instance, Jack explained,

> I struggled this year with maintaining the way that I teach and the hours, just like a lack of sleep and spending so much time with the kids—it started to wear on me. I kind of started to lose my love a little bit for teaching, for the youth at my school, and so I just knew that I needed to step out of the classroom for a little bit so I don't get burned out.

Teacher burnout has severe consequences for the replicability of the practices that has led to KIPP's ability to beat the odds on a large scale. This is because burnout leads to teacher turnover, which, among other things, may negatively impact teacher collaboration. High teacher turnover was noted as a problem in the majority of interviews. Colleen noted, "Traditionally, the life of a teacher at our school is two to three years." Jared stated,

> And the thing that we have trouble with on our campus is obviously turnover. In the summer, I see a tremendous number of new teachers. This is starting my fourth summer and I am very much a veteran teacher because very few people stay for longer than a year or two. I feel like the turnover is very high.

Similarly, Aaron noted,

> One of the biggest detriments to the KIPP schooling system is the high turnover rate for teachers . . . It's rare that you would go to a large grouping of KIPP teachers and find a large percentage of them who have taught for more than 3 or 4 years . . . for most KIPP teachers it's their second to third year—I mean these are veteran teachers in the KIPP world, being part of the KIPP school for 2 maybe 3 years, and to me that's a large detriment.

Many teachers expressed their frustration with trying to maintain the school culture with few returning teachers. Colleen stated,

> Last year we had no returning staff members on the fifth grade's team, which was really challenging because it is the most important year of

the school, in that if you mess up with the incoming grade, they're not going to be bought in, etc., etc. So we didn't have any guidance on our team, and it was really difficult.

Colleen indicated that remaining at KIPP was no longer possible because of the toll that teaching this incoming grade had taken. Similarly, Patty discussed the challenges of getting new staff members "up to speed":

This is the third year I've been teaching at this school and almost every teacher I started out with has gone, has left, and the teachers that replaced them have left. Basically in June, it's a new staff and we kind of have to start over on page one with developing culture and keeping things going.

High teacher turnover was evident in the sample: Some of the teachers had already given their notice and were leaving at the end of the 2006–2007 school year, and others reported planning to leave their KIPP schools after the upcoming school year. Other teachers expressed uncertainty about the future of their career, often saying things like "We'll see how this year goes." Seven teachers in the sample either had already made plans to leave or were making plans to leave KIPP in the next year or two. Two teachers said they were unsure how much longer they would remain teaching at KIPP. Only three said that they planned to remain teaching at KIPP indefinitely.

Reasons for leaving ranged from wanting to return to school to pursue a graduate degree, to having to deal with family necessities, to pursing a career in educational administration, to wanting to teach at a more flexible and less time-consuming school. Consistent with the literature on teacher turnover, one teacher cited the following reasons for leaving KIPP and the profession of teaching: low pay, lack of reward, lack of prestige, lack of respect, and lack of intellectual challenge.

A telling piece of evidence indicating that the time commitment was too much for many teachers is that when the teachers in the sample were asked what they would like to change about their job, six of the teachers specifically said that they would change the hours. The teachers also discussed how this would be possible by instituting more flexible scheduling or job sharing or by being more efficient with the school day in order to cut back on hours. Making such changes may help KIPP schools retain teachers. The significant time required to be a KIPP teacher results in a high turnover rate, which many teachers see as detrimental to the school culture and its effectiveness. The majority of teachers did not feel that they could sustain the commitment level required to beat the odds. This raises questions regarding the ability of this model to be replicated on a much broader scale. If there are not enough teachers willing and/or able to complete the number of hours required, this model may not provide the education system with a realistic solution.

These interviews with KIPP teachers highlight ways in which KIPP schools create positive environments for their teachers—environments likely to lead to improved student achievement. But the interviews also reveal detrimental aspects of the KIPP model. On the positive side, KIPP teachers use "best practices" such as data-driven decision making, collaboration among teachers, and the creation of engaging and challenging lessons. Furthermore, the school culture of hard work and dedication among both teachers and students encourages teacher retention. However, on average, KIPP teachers work more hours per day than other teachers, and this significant time commitment results in a high turnover rate, making it difficult to maintain the culture and effectiveness of KIPP schools.

DISCUSSION

KIPP schools have implemented a number of practices that are critical to helping them beat the odds. Moreover, KIPP schools generate and maintain a collegial, cooperative teaching environment with administrative support and additional pay for extended hours, all of which are policies that the literature suggests are helpful in retaining teachers. The teachers interviewed here reported spending extraordinary amounts of time implementing these best practices, and many KIPP teachers questioned their ability to sustain the significant time commitment and corresponding sacrifices to their personal lives required to implement the practices that are needed to beat the odds. The teachers reported that turnover remains high even with the positive environment.

In comparison to national averages, KIPP teachers are working about 14 hr a week more than their counterparts in regular public schools or other charter schools. The average middle school teacher at a traditional public school spends 52 hr and 2 min working each week, and at charter schools the average middle school teacher spends 51 hr and 34 min a week working (National Center for Education Statistics, 2007).[5] This means that KIPP teachers are working more than an extra day each week compared to other middle school teachers.

The fact that KIPP teachers work longer hours than other teachers is not surprising given that more time is built into the KIPP model. The longer hours are an essential piece of the KIPP model and certainly

---

[5]These data come from a question on the 2003–2004 Schools and Staffing Survey from the National Center for Education Statistics, which asked "How many total hours do you spend on ALL teaching and other school-related activities during a typical FULL WEEK at this school?".

contribute to students' achievement gains. The KIPP pillar of More Time states,

> With an extended school day, week, and year, students have more time in the classroom to acquire the academic knowledge and skills that will prepare them for competitive high schools and colleges, as well as more opportunities to engage in diverse extracurricular experiences. (KIPP, n.d.-b)

KIPP schools are successful at improving the reading test scores of their students, but teachers' perceptions of the sustainability of the KIPP model on a personal level call into question the likelihood of successful replication and sustainability on a very large scale. The number of hours required is simply not possible for many, and thus there is a limited supply of teachers who are willing and able to make such a commitment to their school. A short supply of teachers will hinder the replicability of this model.

Teacher reports of working extensive hours and ignoring one's own personal health and social needs may not be a feature of only KIPP schools. Johnson and Landman (2000) noted that "in their intense and shared dedication to the school and students' needs, teachers may ignore or discount their own immediate personal needs and long-term professional interests" (p. 89). They too documented highly successful teachers at other schools who commented that the turnover rates were troubling and that they "[couldn't] keep this pace up" (p. 90). This suggests that although the practices identified by previous research as leading to better than expected student success may be possible, large-scale replication efforts may not be possible because the teachers who carry out this important work are, for the most part, unable to keep up with the pace of the job.

Teacher turnover can be detrimental to the success of students as well. High teacher turnover makes creating and sustaining a positive school culture difficult. The KIPP model requires significant buy-in on the part of the teachers that must be shared with incoming students. If each year begins with many new teachers, it may be difficult for that school to maintain its culture and "KIPP-matize" its students. High turnover certainly puts excess strain on returning teachers, who must bear the brunt of the acculturation process. Currently, however, teacher churn seems to be built into the design of the KIPP model.

If the KIPP model is not replicable on a large scale because of the short supply of saints willing to make extensive commitments to their jobs and sacrifices to their personal lives, is it truly a successful school reform? The KIPP model has been successful for a small network of schools, but that success may not easily be translated into systemic education reform. KIPP has claimed that its success will prompt "widespread expectation that public schools everywhere can help students overcome disadvantages to succeed academically and in life" (KIPP, 2003, p. 3). But can such widespread expectations be met if there is a limited pool of teachers who are willing and able to do such intense work? This research illuminates what it takes teachers and schools to "help students overcome disadvantages to succeed academically" and finds that it takes so much that most teachers are able to give it only a few years. It seems unlikely that schools everywhere could adopt this model. Although previous research has identified effective schools practices, the interviews here suggest that implementing these practices takes a tremendous toll on the teachers. Teachers question their ability to sustain the work and acknowledge that widespread adoption of these practices is not possible.

CONCLUSION

As evidenced in this sample, many KIPP teachers are not career KIPP teachers. This does not currently seem to be problematic for the KIPP model. However, as it expands, this issue will become more pressing. Although there may be nothing inherent in the KIPP model that deters individuals from a career in teaching, it seems that KIPP schools often attract teachers who are willing to give 100% of themselves but only for a short period of time. Colleen explained that the question regarding the sustainability of teachers who implement these effective practices was really not pertinent to the KIPP model:

> The mission of the KIPP school is to serve children who are traditionally underserved . . . I think the attitude is that these students deserve the very best and if we burn through teachers, then we burn through teachers. I think the project here is not about teacher sustainability. I think the project is about how we're going to do whatever it takes to educate these kids as best as we can and if that means teachers leave after two years, teachers leave after two years.

But although Colleen's sense of the model may be correct, is this what it takes to raise the reading achievement of poor and minority children? Does improving the education of poor children require a revolving door of short-term saints who sacrifice a few years of their young adult lives to ensure that poor children receive the education they deserve and so desperately need? Furthermore, if it were to be expected that these effective practices would be implemented on a very broad scale, it seems unlikely that there would be enough teachers to fill these positions. Surely, this is not the only answer to beat the odds. However, too often political leaders use these examples as proof that if only teachers would work harder, they could solve the problems of urban public schools and close the reading achievement gap.

Although success has certainly been achieved by these teachers who work extraordinarily hard, the emphasis on expecting schools to solve the larger economic and social problems of this country alone will only result in burnout and shortages. KIPP schools have been able to overcome many of the obstacles their students face; however, the price is extraordinarily high for the teachers, and their ability to do the job is short lived at best. Sarah struggled with this and noted,

> I guess the justification [for the additional hours] is that often times there are households where both parents are working and if they weren't with us, they would be in some center until 5:00 or 5:30 p.m. So given those options, I'd rather have them be with me.

But the options this teacher currently faces need not be so limited. Instead of pursuing school reform alone and expecting schools and teachers to fill these many roles and "do it all," policymakers and political leaders should be focusing on building communities that beat the odds through a wide array of social and economic reforms that support children's health and social development both inside of school and out.

Given the myriad of obstacles minority and poor children face, schools and teachers can only be expected to be part of the solution. The goal should not be for schools alone to beat the odds with teachers sacrificing their own lives to accomplish this. Rather, experts should work to reform all institutions that contribute to a student's success, including housing, health, economic, and educational institutions.

If the teachers interviewed here are typical, and there is no reason to believe that they are not, then finding enough teachers who are willing to go to such extraordinary lengths to staff all of the schools in which students are struggling to learn to read seems highly unlikely. Relying upon this model alone to solve the problems of failing schools is likely to result in disappointment and can only distract from the larger work that must be done.

REFERENCES

Anderson, A. B., & DeCesare, D. (2006). *Opening closed doors: Lesson's from Colorado's first independent charter school.* Denver, CO: Augenblick, Palaich & Associates.

Bush, G. W. (2003, July). *President discusses education reform in DC.* Retrieved from http://www.whitehouse.gov/news/releases/2003/07/20030701-3.html

Certo, J. L., & Fox, J. E. (2002). Retaining quality teachers. *The High School Journal, 86*(1), 57–75.

Chubb, J., & Loveless, T. (Eds.). (2002). *Bridging the achievement gap.* Washington, DC: Brookings Institution.

Coleman, J. S., Campbell, E. Q., Hobson, C. J., McPartland, J., Mood, A. M., Weinfeld, F. D., & York, R. L. (1966). *Equality of educational opportunity: Summary report*. Washington, DC: U.S. Department of Health, Education, and Welfare; Office of Education/National Center for Education Statistics.

Converse, J. M., & Presser, S. (1986). *Survey questions: Handcrafting the standardized questionnaire*. Thousand Oaks, CA: Sage.

Cunningham, P. M. (2006). High-poverty schools that beat the odds. *The Reading Teacher, 60*, 382–385.

Darling-Hammond, L. (2003). Keeping good teachers: Why it matters, what leaders can do. *Educational Leadership, 60*(8), 6–13.

David, J., Woodworth, K., Grant, E., Guha, R., Lopez-Torkos, A., & Young, V. (2006). *Bay Area KIPP schools: A study of early implementation, first year report 2004–05*. Menlo Park, CA: SRI International.

Doran, H. C., & Drury, D. W. (2002). *Evaluating success: KIPP educational program evaluation*. Washington, DC: New American Schools.

Duncan, G. L., & Seymour, P. H. (2000). Socioeconomic differences in foundation level literacy. *British Journal of Psychology, 91*, 145–166.

Education Policy Institute. (2005). *Focus on results: An academic impact analysis of the Knowledge Is Power Program (KIPP)*. Virginia Beach, VA: Education Policy Institute International.

Education Trust. (2003). *African American achievement in America*. Retrieved from http://www2.edtrust.org/NR/rdonlyres/47501795-973A-490A-9345-A03110A9651E/0/AchievementAfricanAmericanveryfinal.ppt

Fuller, H. (2001). *Freedom to Learn conference keynote remarks*. Retrieved from http://www.charterfriends.org/freedom.html#fuller

Gallagher, B. M., & Ross, S. M. (2005). *Analysis of year 2 (2003–2004) student achievement outcomes for the Memphis KIPP DIAMOND Academy*. Memphis, TN: University of Memphis, Center for Research in Education Policy.

Gardner, D. P. (1983). *A nation at risk: The imperative for education reform*. Washington, DC: U.S. Government Printing Office.

Guarino, C. M., Santibanez, L., & Daley, G. A. (2006). Teacher recruitment and retention: A review of the recent empirical literature. *Review of Educational Research, 76*, 173–208.

Hart, B., & Risley, T. (1995). *Meaningful differences in the everyday experiences of young American children*. Baltimore, MD: Brookes.

Hoffman, J. (1991). Teacher and school effects in learning to read. In R. Barr, M. Kamil, P. Mosenthal, & P. D. Pearson (Eds.), *Handbook of reading research* (Vol. 2, pp. 911–950). New York, NY: Longman.

Ingersoll, R. M. (2001). Teacher turnover and teacher shortages: An organizational analysis. *American Educational Research Journal, 38*, 499–534.

Ingersoll, R. M. (2003). *Is there really a teacher shortage?* Retrieved from http://www.gse.upenn.edu/inpress/Is%20There%20Really%20a%20Teacher%20Shortage.pdf

Jencks, C., & Phillips, M. (Eds.). (1998). *The black-white test score gap*. Washington, DC: Brookings Institution.

Johnson, S. M., & Birkeland, S. E. (2002). *Pursuing "a sense of success": New teachers explain their career decisions*. Retrieved from http://www.gse.harvard.edu/~ngt/Johnson_Birkeland_Oct_2002.pdf

Johnson, S. M., Birkeland, S., Kardos, S. M., Kauffman, D., Liu, E., & Peske, H. G. (2001). *Retaining the next generation of teachers: The importance of school-based support.* Retrieved from http://www.physics.ohio-state.edu/~jossem/REF/99.pdf

Johnson, S. M., & Landman, J. (2000). Sometimes bureaucracy has its charms: The working conditions of teachers in deregulated schools. *Teachers College Record, 102*(1), 85–124.

KIPP. (2003). *KIPP: 2003 report card.* San Francisco, CA: KIPP Foundation.

KIPP. (2006). *KIPP: 2006 report card.* San Francisco, CA: KIPP Foundation.

KIPP. (n.d.-a). *About KIPP: Overview.* Retrieved from http://www.kipp.org/01/

KIPP. (n.d.-b). *About KIPP: Five pillars.* Retrieved from http://www.kipp.org/01/fivepillars.cfm

KIPP. (n.d.-c). *About KIPP: What is a KIPP school.* Retrieved from http://www.kipp.org/01/whatisakippschool.cfm

Langdon, C. A. (1996). The third Phi Delta Kappa poll of teachers' attitudes toward the public schools. *Phi Delta Kappan, 78*, 244–251.

Langer, J. A. (2001). Beating the odds: Teaching middle and high school students to read and write well. *American Educational Research Journal, 38*, 837–880.

Lareau, A. (2000). *Home advantage: Social class and parental intervention in elementary education.* New York, NY: Rowman & Littlefield.

Malloy, C. L., & Wohlstetter, P. (2003). Working conditions in charter schools: What's the appeal for teachers? *Education and Urban Society, 35*, 219–241.

Miles, M., & Huberman, M. (1984). *Qualitative data analysis: A sourcebook of new methods.* Beverly Hills, CA: Sage.

National Center for Education Statistics. (2007). *Schools and staffing survey, 2003–2004, public teacher file.* Retrieved from http://nces.ed.gov/dasol/index.asp

National Commission on Teaching. (1997). *Doing what matters most: Investing in quality teaching.* New York, NY: Author. (ERIC Document Reproduction Service No. ED415 183)

Ogbu, J. (2003). *Black American students in an affluent suburb: A study of academic disengagement.* Mahwah, NJ: Erlbaum.

Perie, M., Moran, R., & Lutkus, A. D. (2005). *NAEP 2004 trends in academic progress: Three decades of student performance in reading and mathematics* (National Center for Education Statistics Report No. 2005–464). Washington, DC: National Center for Education Statistics.

Puma, M. J., Karweit, N., Price, C., Ricciuti, A., Thompson, W., Vaden-Kiernan, M., & Kiernan, M. (1997). *Prospects: Student outcomes. Final report.* Washington, DC: U.S. Department of Education, Planning and Evaluation Services.

Rice, J. K. (2003). *Teacher quality: Understanding the effectiveness of teacher attributes.* Washington, DC: Economic Policy Institute.

Rothstein, R. (2004). *Class and schools: Using social, economic and educational reform to close the black-white achievement gap.* Washington, DC: Economic Policy Institute.

Sanders, W. L., & Horn, S. P. (1998). Research findings from the Tennessee value-added assessment system (TVAAS) database: Implications for educational evaluation and research. *Journal of Personnel Evaluation in Education, 12*, 247–256.

Snow, C. E., Burns, S., & Griffin, P. (1998). *Preventing reading difficulties in young children*. Washington, DC: National Academies Press.

Taylor, B. M., Pearson, P. D., Clark, K., & Walpole, S. (2000). Effective schools and accomplished teachers: Lessons about primary-grade reading instruction in low-income schools. *Elementary School Journal, 101*, 121–164.

Taylor, B. M., Pearson, P. D., Peterson, D. S., & Rodriguez, M. C. (2003). Reading growth in high-poverty classrooms: The influence of teacher practices that encourage cognitive engagement in literacy learning. *Elementary School Journal, 104*(1), 4–28.

Taylor, B. M., Pearson, P. D., Peterson, D. S., & Rodriguez, M. C. (2005). The CIERA school change framework: An evidence-based approach to professional development and school reading improvement. *Reading Research Quarterly, 40*(1), 40–69.

Taylor, B. M., Pressley, M., & Pearson, P. D. (2002). Research-supported characteristics of teachers and schools that promote reading achievement. In B. M. Taylor & P. D. Pearson (Eds.), *Teaching reading: Effective schools, accomplished teachers* (pp. 361–374). Mahwah, NJ: Erlbaum.

Thernstrom, A., & Thernstrom, S. (2003). *No excuses: Closing the racial gap in learning*. New York, NY: Simon & Schuster.

Tye, B. B., & O'Brien, L. (2002). Why are experienced teachers leaving the profession? *Phi Delta Kappan, 84*, 24–32.

Wright, S. P., Horn, S. P., & Sanders, W. L. (1997). Teacher and classroom context effects on student achievement: Implications for teacher evaluation. *Journal of Personnel Evaluation in Education, 11*(1), 57–67.

APPENDIX

The KIPP Model Five Pillars

1. *High Expectations*: KIPP schools have clearly defined and measurable high expectations for academic achievement and conduct that make no excuses based on the students' backgrounds. Students, parents, teachers, and staff create and reinforce a culture of achievement and support through a range of formal and informal rewards and consequences for academic performance and behavior.

2. *Choice and Commitment*: Students, their parents, and the faculty of each KIPP school choose to participate in the program. No one is assigned or forced to attend a KIPP school. Everyone must make and uphold a commitment to the school and to each other to put in the time and effort required to achieve success.

3. *More Time*: KIPP schools know that there are no shortcuts when it comes to success in academics and life. With an extended school day, week, and year, students have more time in the classroom to acquire the academic knowledge and skills that will prepare them for competitive high schools

and colleges, as well as more opportunities to engage in diverse extracurricular experiences.

4. *Power to Lead*: The principals of KIPP schools are effective academic and organizational leaders who understand that great schools require great school leaders. They have control over their school budget and personnel. They are free to swiftly move dollars or make staffing changes, allowing them maximum effectiveness in helping students learn.

5. *Focus on Results*: KIPP schools relentlessly focus on high student performance on standardized tests and other objective measures. Just as there are no shortcuts, there are no excuses. Students are expected to achieve a level of academic performance that will enable them to succeed at the nation's best high schools and colleges.

Source. KIPP (n.d.-b).

Index

Page numbers in *Italics* represent tables.
Page numbers in **Bold** represent figures.

9781032930459